Qualifications and Credit Framework (QCF)

AQ2013 (FA2014)
LEVEL 4 DIPLOMA IN ACCOUNTING

## QUESTION BANK

Business Tax

2014 Edition

For assessments from January 2015

Second edition August 2014
ISBN 9781 4727 0942 4

Previous edition August 2013
ISBN 9781 4727 0354 5

**British Library Cataloguing-in-Publication Data**
A catalogue record for this book is available from the British Library

**Published by**
BPP Learning Media Ltd
BPP House
Aldine Place
London W12 8AA

www.bpp.com/learningmedia

**Printed in the United Kingdom by Martins of Berwick**
Sea View Works
Spittal
Berwick-Upon-Tweed
TD15 1RS

# CONTENTS

# A NOTE ABOUT COPYRIGHT

Dear Customer

What does the little © mean and why does it matter?

Your market-leading BPP books, course materials and e-learning materials do not write and update themselves. People write them on their own behalf or as employees of an organisation that invests in this activity. Copyright law protects their livelihoods. It does so by creating rights over the use of the content.

Breach of copyright is a form of theft – as well as being a criminal offence in some jurisdictions, it is potentially a serious breach of professional ethics.

With current technology, things might seem a bit hazy but, basically, without the express permission of BPP Learning Media:

- Photocopying our materials is a breach of copyright

- Scanning, ripcasting or conversion of our digital materials into different file formats, uploading them to facebook or emailing them to your friends is a breach of copyright

You can, of course, sell your books, in the form in which you have bought them – once you have finished with them. (Is this fair to your fellow students? We update for a reason). Please note the e-products are sold on a single user licence basis: we do not supply 'unlock' codes to people who have bought them secondhand.

And what about outside the UK? BPP Learning Media strives to make our materials available at prices students can afford by local printing arrangements, pricing policies and partnerships which are clearly listed on our website. A tiny minority ignore this and indulge in criminal activity by illegally photocopying our material or supporting organisations that do. If they act illegally and unethically in one area, can you really trust them?

# INTRODUCTION

This is BPP Learning Media's AAT Question Bank for Business Tax. It is part of a suite of ground-breaking resources produced by BPP Learning Media for the AAT's assessments under the Qualification and Credit Framework.

The Business Tax assessment will be **computer assessed**. As well as being available in the traditional paper format, this **Question Bank is available in an online environment** containing tasks similar to those you will encounter in the AAT's testing environment. BPP Learning Media believe that the best way to practise for an online assessment is in an online environment. However, if you are unable to practise in the online environment you will find that all tasks in the paper Question Bank have been written in a style that is as close as possible to the style that you will be presented with in your online assessment.

This Question Bank has been written in conjunction with the BPP Text, and has been carefully designed to enable students to practise all of the learning outcomes and assessment criteria for the units that make up Business Tax. It is fully up to date for Finance Act 2014 and reflects both the AAT's unit guide and sample assessment(s) provided by the AAT.

This Question Bank contains these key features:

- Tasks corresponding to each chapter of the Text. Some tasks are designed for learning purposes, others are of assessment standard.

- The AAT's sample assessment(s) and answers for Business Tax and further BPP practice assessments.

The emphasis in all tasks and assessments is on the practical application of the skills acquired.

## VAT

You may find tasks throughout this Question Bank that need you to calculate or be aware of a rate of VAT. This is stated at 20% in these examples and questions.

## APPROACHING THE ASSESSMENT

When you sit the assessment it is very important that you follow the on screen instructions. This means you need to carefully read the instructions, both on the introduction screens and during specific tasks.

When you access the assessment you should be presented with an introductory screen with information similar to that shown below (taken from the introductory screen from the AAT's AQ2013 Sample Assessment for Business Tax).

*We have provided the following sample assessment to help you familiarise yourself with AAT's e-assessment environment. It is designed to demonstrate as many as possible of the question types you may find in a live assessment. It is not designed to be used on its own to determine whether you are ready for a live assessment.*

*This assessment comprises 11 tasks.*

*You should attempt and aim to complete EVERY task in EACH section.*

*Each task is independent. You will not need to refer to your answers to previous tasks.*

*Read every task carefully to make sure you understand what is required.*

*Please note that in this assessment only your responses to task 1, 3, 4, 5, 6 and 9 will be marked.*

*Equivalents of tasks 2, 7, 8 and 10 will be human marked in the live assessment.*

*Where the date is relevant, it is given in the task data.*

*Both minus signs and brackets can be used to indicate negative numbers UNLESS task instructions say otherwise.*

*You must use a full stop to indicate a decimal point.*

*For example, write 100.57 NOT 100,57 or 100 57*

*You may use a comma to indicate a number in the thousands, but you don't have to.*

*For example, 10000 and 10,000 are both OK.*

*Other indicators are not compatible with the computer-marked system.*

*There are two tables of tax data provided in this assessment. You can access these at any point by clicking on the buttons found in every task. The buttons will appear at the top of each task, and look like this:*

*When you click on a button, the table will appear in a pop-up window. You can then move or close the window.*

*When you move on to a new task, you will have to re-open a window to see the data again.*

*The taxation data is also available in this introduction, and can be accessed at any time during the assessment by clicking on the introduction button on the bottom left of the assessment window.*

The actual instructions will vary depending on the subject you are studying for. It is very important you read the instructions on the introductory screen and apply them in the assessment. You don't want to lose marks when you know the correct answer just because you have not entered it in the right format.

In general, the rules set out in the AAT Sample Assessments for the subject you are studying for will apply in the real assessment, but you should again read the information on this screen in the real assessment carefully just to make sure. This screen may also confirm the VAT rate used if applicable.

A full stop is needed to indicate a decimal point. We would recommend using minus signs to indicate negative numbers and leaving out the comma signs to indicate thousands, as this results in a lower number of key strokes and less margin for error when working under time pressure. Having said that, you can use whatever is easiest for you as long as you operate within the rules set out for your particular assessment.

You have to show competence throughout the assessment and you should therefore complete all of the tasks. Don't leave questions unanswered.

In some assessments written or complex tasks may be human marked. In this case you are given a blank space or table to enter your answer into. You are told in the assessments which tasks these are (note: there may be none if all answers are marked by the computer).

If these involve calculations, it is a good idea to decide in advance how you are going to lay out your answers to such tasks by practising answering them on a word document, and certainly you should try all such tasks in this question bank and in the AAT's environment using the sample/practice assessments.

When asked to fill in tables, or gaps, never leave any blank even if you are unsure of the answer. Fill in your best estimate.

Note that for some assessments where there is a lot of scenario information or tables of data provided (e.g. tax tables), you may need to access these via 'pop-ups'. Instructions will be provided on how you can bring up the necessary data during the assessment.

Finally, take note of any task specific instructions once you are in the assessment. For example you may be asked to enter a date in a certain format or to enter a number to a certain number of decimal places.

Remember you can practise the BPP questions in this question bank in an online environment on our dedicated AAT Online page. On the same page is a link to the current AAT Sample Assessment(s) as well.

If you have any comments about this book, please e-mail ianblackmore@bpp.com or write to Ian Blackmore, AAT Range Manager, BPP Learning Media Ltd, BPP House, Aldine Place, London W12 8AA

## SPECIFIC TOPIC LIST

The practice tasks are grouped according to the main topics assessed in Business Tax. This table gives you a list of tasks dealing with specific topics to enable you to focus your task practice.

| Topic | Practice tasks |
| --- | --- |
| Badges of trade | 1.1 |
| Adjustment of profit for sole trader | 1.2, 1.3 |
| Adjustment of profit for company | 1.5, 1.6 |
| Self employment tax return | 1.4 |
| Revenue or capital expenditure | 2.1 |
| Capital allowances for sole trader | 2.2, 2.3. 2.4 |
| Capital allowances for company | 2.5 |
| Basis of assessment for sole trader | 3.1, 3.2, 3.3, 3.4 |
| Partnership allocation of profits | 3.5, 3.6, 3.7, 3.8 |
| Basis of assessment for partners | 3.6, 6.5 |
| Partnership tax return | 3.9 |
| Long period of account | 4.1, 4.2 |
| Corporation tax calculation | 4.3, 4.4, 4.5, 4.6 |
| Corporation tax return | 4.7 |
| Losses for sole trader | 5.1, 5.2, 5.3, 5.4 |
| Losses for company | 5.5, 5.6, 5.7, 5.8, 5.9 |
| National insurance contributions | 6.1, 6.2, 6.3, 6.4, 6.5 |
| Filing date for return | 7.1 |
| Penalties and interest | 7.3, 7.4, 7.5, 7.6, 7.7 |
| Payment of tax by individuals | 7.2, 7.9 |
| Payment of tax by companies | 7.8, 7.9 |
| Chargeable gains definitions | 8.1, 8.2, 8.12 |
| Calculation of gains for individuals | 8.3 |
| Capital losses | 8.4, 8.5, 8.6, 8.8, 8.9 |
| Capital gains tax payable | 8.4, 8.6, 8.7 |
| Calculation of gains for companies | 8.10, 8.11 |
| Part disposals | 9.1, 9.7 |
| Chattels | 9.2, 9.3, 9.4, 9.8 |
| Connected persons | 9.5, 9.6 |
| Share disposals by individuals | 10.1, 10.2, 10.3 |
| Share disposals by companies | 10.4, 10.5, 10.6 |
| Entrepreneurs' relief | 11.1, 11.2 |
| Gift relief | 11.3, 11.4 |
| Rollover relief | 11.5, 11.6, 11.7 |

# Question bank

# Business Tax – Practice tasks

## Adjustment to profits

### Task 1.1

**This style of task is human marked in the live assessment.**

When deciding whether a trade is being carried on, HM Revenue and Customs is often guided by the badges of trade.

**Write a memo to a client who is concerned they may be trading, explaining what is meant by the term badges of trade.**

| | |
|---|---|
| **From:** | AAT student |
| **To:** | A Client |
| **Date:** | 14 June 2015 |
| **Subject:** | Badges of trade |

This page is for the continuation of your memo. You may not need all of it.

## Task 1.2

The statement of profit or loss for Mr Jelly for the year ended 31 December 2014 shows:

| | £ | | £ |
|---|---|---|---|
| Staff wages | 12,500 | Gross profit from trading account | 20,000 |
| Light and heat | 162 | | |
| Motor car expenses | 350 | | |
| Postage, stationery and telephone | 100 | | |
| Repairs and renewals | 450 | | |
| Irrecoverable debts | 238 | | |
| Miscellaneous expenses | 300 | | |
| Depreciation charge | 600 | | |
| Profit for the year | 5,300 | | |
| | 20,000 | | 20,000 |

The following information is also relevant:

(1) The staff wages include £260 paid to Mr Jelly.

(2) One-seventh of the motor expenses relates to private motoring.

(3) Repairs and renewals comprise:

| | £ |
|---|---|
| Painting shop internally | 129 |
| Plant repairs | 220 |
| Building extension to stockroom | 101 |
| | 450 |

(4) Irrecoverable debt provisions

| 2014 | | £ | 2014 | | £ |
|---|---|---|---|---|---|
| | | | Jan 1 | Balances b/f | |
| Dec 31 | Balances c/f | | | General | 200 |
| | General | 400 | | Specific | 360 |
| | Specific | 398 | | | |
| | | | Dec 31 | Statement of profit or loss | 238 |
| | | 798 | | | 798 |

(5) Miscellaneous expenses include:

| | £ |
|---|---|
| Donations – Oxfam | 10 |
| Advertising | 115 |
| Customer entertaining | 90 |
| Christmas gifts – ten bottles of gin and whisky | 70 |
| Legal expenses re debt collecting | 15 |
| | 300 |

**Using the proforma layout provided, compute Mr Jelly's taxable trading profit for the year ended 31 December 2014. Input 0 (zero) if necessary, in order to fill in all unshaded boxes.**

| | £ | £ |
|---|---|---|
| Profit for the year per accounts | | |
| | Add | Deduct |
| staff wages | | |
| Mr Jelly's salary | | |
| light and heat | | |
| motor expenses | | |
| postage, stationery and telephone | | |
| painting shop internally | | |
| plant repairs | | |
| stockroom extension | | |
| Irrecoverable debts - provision | | |
| donations | | |
| advertising | | |
| entertaining | | |
| gifts | | |
| legal expenses | | |
| depreciation charge | | |
| Total net adjustments | | |
| Taxable trading profit | | |

## Task 1.3

Decide how each of the following items would be treated in the tax computation of a sole trader. Tick ONE box per line.

| | Allow ✓ | Disallow and add back ✓ | Not taxable so deduct ✓ |
|---|---|---|---|
| Increase in specific provision | | | |
| Decrease in general provision | | | |
| Depreciation charge | | | |
| Cocktail party held for customers | | | |
| Political donation | | | |
| Employees salary | | | |
| Repair to factory roof | | | |

## Task 1.4

**This style of task is human marked in the live assessment.**

Graham has carried on business for many years making up accounts to 31 March each year.

The following information is relevant to his period of account to 31 March 2015:

| | £ |
|---|---|
| Revenue | 150,000 |
| Cost of goods bought | 25,000 |
| Heating | 1,200 |
| Insurance | 560 |
| Office costs | 1,700 |
| Bank charges | 150 |
| Accountancy and legal costs (£500 disallowable as relates to capital) | 1,650 |
| Goods taken for own use (market value) | 750 |
| New car ($CO_2$ emissions 170 g/km) | 19,000 |

# Using this information, complete the self-employment page below.

## Business expenses

Please read the *Self-employment (full) notes* before filling in this section.

| Total expenses | Disallowable expenses |
|---|---|
| If your annual turnover was below £81,000 you may just put your total expenses in box 31 | Use this column if the figures in boxes 17 to 30 include disallowable amounts |

**17** Cost of goods bought for resale or goods used

£ · 0 0

**32**

£ · 0 0

**18** Construction industry – *payments to subcontractors*

£ · 0 0

**33**

£ · 0 0

**19** Wages, salaries and other staff costs

£ · 0 0

**34**

£ · 0 0

**20** Car, van and travel expenses

£ · 0 0

**35**

£ · 0 0

**21** Rent, rates, power and insurance costs

£ · 0 0

**36**

£ · 0 0

**22** Repairs and renewals of property and equipment

£ · 0 0

**37**

£ · 0 0

**23** Phone, fax, stationery and other office costs

£ · 0 0

**38**

£ · 0 0

**24** Advertising and business entertainment costs

£ · 0 0

**39**

£ · 0 0

**25** Interest on bank and other loans

£ · 0 0

**40**

£ · 0 0

**26** Bank, credit card and other financial charges

£ · 0 0

**41**

£ · 0 0

**27** Irrecoverable debts written off

£ · 0 0

**42**

£ · 0 0

**28** Accountancy, legal and other professional fees

£ · 0 0

**43**

£ · 0 0

**29** Depreciation and loss/profit on sale of assets

£ · 0 0

**44**

£ · 0 0

**30** Other business expenses

£ · 0 0

**45**

£ · 0 0

**31** Total expenses (total of boxes 17 to 30)

£ · 0 0

**46** Total disallowable expenses (total of boxes 32 to 45)

£ · 0 0

SA103F 2014        Page SEF 2

# Task 1.5

Geronimo Ltd's summarised statement of profit or loss for the year ended 31 March 2015 is as follows:

|  | £ | £ |
|---|---|---|
| *Gross profit* |  | 925,940 |
| *Operating expenses* |  |  |
| Depreciation charge | 83,420 |  |
| Gifts (Note 1) | 2,850 |  |
| Professional fees (Note 2) | 14,900 |  |
| Repairs and renewals (Note 3) | 42,310 |  |
| Other expenses (all allowable) | 165,980 |  |
|  |  | (309,460) |
| *Operating profit* |  | 616,480 |
| *Income from investments* |  |  |
| Debenture interest (Note 4) | 24,700 |  |
| Bank interest (Note 4) | 4,800 |  |
| Dividends (Note 5) | 56,000 |  |
|  |  | 85,500 |
|  |  | 701,980 |
| *Interest payable on loans for trading purposes* |  | (45,000) |
| *Profit for the year before taxation* |  | 656,980 |

*Note 1 – Gifts*

Gifts are as follows:

|  | £ |
|---|---|
| Qualifying charitable donation | 1,900 |
| Donation to local charity (Geronimo Ltd received free advertising In the charity's magazine) | 50 |
| Gifts to customers (food hampers costing £30 each) | 900 |
|  | 2,850 |

*Note 2 – Professional fees*

Professional fees are as follows:

|  | £ |
|---|---|
| Accountancy and audit fee | 4,100 |
| Legal fees in connection with the renewal of a 20-year property lease | 2,400 |
| Legal fees in connection with the issue of a debenture loan for trade purposes | 8,400 |
|  | 14,900 |

*Note 3 – Repairs and renewals*

The figure of £42,310 for repairs includes £6,200 for replacing part of a wall that was knocked down by a lorry, and £12,200 for initial repairs to an office building that was acquired during the year ended 31 March 2015. The office building was not usable until the repairs were carried out, and this fact was represented by a reduced purchase price.

*Note 4*

The bank interest and the debenture interest were both received on non-trade investments.

*Note 5 – Dividends received*

The dividends were received from other companies. The figure of £56,000 is the actual amount received.

*Note 6 – Capital allowances*

Capital allowances for the year have been calculated as £13,200.

**Using the proforma layout provided, calculate Geronimo Ltd's taxable trading profit for the year ended 31 March 2015. Use brackets for deductions and insert 0 (zero) if necessary, in order to fill in all unshaded boxes.**

| | £ | £ |
|---|---|---|
| Profit per accounts | | 656,980 |
| | Add | Deduct |
| depreciation charge | | |
| qualifying charitable donation | | |
| donation to local charity | | |
| gifts to customers | | |
| accountancy and audit fee | | |
| legal fees – renewal of 20 year lease | | |
| legal fees – issue of debenture | | |
| repairs – knocked down wall | | |
| initial repairs to office | | |
| other expenses | | |
| debenture interest | | |
| bank interest | | |
| dividends | | |
| capital allowances | | |
| interest payable on trading loans | | |
| Net adjustments | | |
| Taxable trading profit | | |

## Task 1.6

Decide how each of the following items would be treated in the tax computation of a company with respect to its trading profits. Tick ONE box per line.

| | Allow ✓ | Disallow and add back ✓ | Not taxable as trading income so deduct ✓ |
|---|---|---|---|
| Dividends received from an unconnected company | | | |
| Profit on sale of shares | | | |
| Running costs of car with 20% private use by an employee | | | |
| Parking fine of director | | | |
| Capital allowances | | | |
| Director's salary | | | |
| Bank interest received | | | |

## Capital allowances

### Task 2.1

For the following items of expenditure, tick if they are revenue or capital:

| | Revenue | Capital |
|---|---|---|
| Purchase of machinery | ☐ | ☐ |
| Rent paid for premises | ☐ | ☐ |
| Insurance of premises | ☐ | ☐ |
| Repairs to roof of factory | ☐ | ☐ |
| New extension to shop | ☐ | ☐ |
| Purchase of new car for owner | ☐ | ☐ |
| Legal fees relating to purchase of new factory | ☐ | ☐ |
| Payment of staff wages | ☐ | ☐ |
| Accountancy costs | ☐ | ☐ |
| Redecoration of shop | ☐ | ☐ |

### Task 2.2

**This style of task is human marked in the live assessment.**

Bodie, a sole trader, makes up his accounts to 5 April each year. The value of the main pool as at 6 April 2014 was £38,500.

His expenditure, all qualifying for capital allowances, has been as follows:

| Date | | £ |
|---|---|---|
| 14 July 2014 | Office furniture | 23,800 |
| 30 March 2015 | Mercedes car – $CO_2$ emissions 120g/km | 18,000 |
| 31 March 2015 | Car – $CO_2$ emissions 100g/km | 8,000 |
| 2 April 2015 | Machinery | 31,000 |

The Mercedes was for the proprietor's own use (20% private), while the other car was for an employee.

Machinery which had been acquired for £7,000 was sold for £3,000 on 29 March 2015.

Using the proforma layout provided, calculate capital allowances for the year ending 5 April 2015.

| | | | | |
|---|---|---|---|---|
| | | | | |
| | | | | |
| | | | | |
| | | | | |
| | | | | |
| | | | | |
| | | | | |
| | | | | |
| | | | | |
| | | | | |
| | | | | |
| | | | | |
| | | | | |
| | | | | |
| | | | | |
| | | | | |
| | | | | |
| | | | | |
| | | | | |
| | | | | |
| | | | | |
| | | | | |

## Task 2.3

**This style of task is human marked in the live assessment.**

Wolfgang commences to trade on 1 January 2014. During his first year, he incurs the following expenditure:

| | | £ |
|---|---|---|
| 6 May 2014 | Machinery | 455,750 |
| 6 July 2014 | Car with $CO_2$ emissions of 90g/km | 8,000 |
| 31 August 2014 | Car with $CO_2$ emissions of 125g/km | 10,500 |

Using the proforma layout provided, compute the capital allowance available to Wolfgang for the year ended 31 December 2014.

| | | | | |
|---|---|---|---|---|
| | | | | |
| | | | | |
| | | | | |
| | | | | |
| | | | | |
| | | | | |
| | | | | |
| | | | | |
| | | | | |
| | | | | |
| | | | | |
| | | | | |
| | | | | |
| | | | | |
| | | | | |
| | | | | |
| | | | | |
| | | | | |
| | | | | |
| | | | | |
| | | | | |
| | | | | |
| | | | | |
| | | | | |

## Task 2.4

**This style of task is human marked in the live assessment.**

Rachel is a sole trader making up accounts to 31 March each year.

On 1 April 2014, the brought forward balances on her plant and machinery were as follows:

|  | £ |
|---|---|
| Main pool | 120,000 |
| Car – private use 30% by Rachel | 21,000 |
| Special rate pool | 17,500 |

She sold the car she used privately for £16,000 on 10 August 2014 and bought another car (CO$_2$ emissions 170g/km) on the same day for £25,000, which also had 30% private use by her.

**Using the proforma layout provided, calculate the capital allowances available in the year to 31 March 2015.**

|  |  |  |  |  |  |
|---|---|---|---|---|---|
|  |  |  |  |  |  |
|  |  |  |  |  |  |
|  |  |  |  |  |  |
|  |  |  |  |  |  |
|  |  |  |  |  |  |
|  |  |  |  |  |  |
|  |  |  |  |  |  |
|  |  |  |  |  |  |
|  |  |  |  |  |  |
|  |  |  |  |  |  |
|  |  |  |  |  |  |
|  |  |  |  |  |  |
|  |  |  |  |  |  |
|  |  |  |  |  |  |
|  |  |  |  |  |  |

## Task 2.5

**This style of task is human marked in the live assessment.**

At the end of the period of account to 31 March 2014, the value of the main pool in Green Ltd's tax computations was £106,000.

On 1 January 2015 a car costing £14,000 was acquired. The $CO_2$ emissions of the car were 170 g/km, and was used privately 30% of the time by the Finance Director.

There were no other purchases or sales during the year. The company had always prepared accounts to 31 March.

**Using the proforma layout provided, calculate the capital allowances available in the year ended 31 March 2015.**

|  |  |  |  |
|---|---|---|---|
|  |  |  |  |
|  |  |  |  |
|  |  |  |  |
|  |  |  |  |
|  |  |  |  |
|  |  |  |  |
|  |  |  |  |
|  |  |  |  |
|  |  |  |  |
|  |  |  |  |
|  |  |  |  |
|  |  |  |  |
|  |  |  |  |

# Basis periods and partnerships

## Task 3.1

Rachel commenced in business as a fashion designer on 1 January 2013, and made up her first accounts to 30 April 2014. Her profit for the period, adjusted for taxation, was £33,000.

**Her first tax year is:**

| |
|---|
| |

**Her taxable profits in her first tax year of trading are:**

£ | |

**Her taxable profits in her second tax year of trading are:**

£ | |

**Her taxable profits in her third tax year of trading are:**

£ | |

**Overlap profits are:**

£ | |

## Task 3.2

Mr Phone commenced trading on 1 July 2012 making up accounts to 31 May each year.

Profits are:

| | £ |
|---|---|
| 1 July 2012 to 31 May 2013 | 22,000 |
| Year ended 31 May 2014 | 18,000 |
| Year ended 31 May 2015 | 30,000 |

**Mr Phone's basis period for 2012/13 runs from:** (insert the date as xx/xx/xxxx)

| |
|---|
| |

**to:**

| |
|---|
| |

**Mr Phone's basis period for 2013/14 runs from:** (insert the date as xx/xx/xxxx)

| |
|---|
| |

**to:**

[ ]

**His taxable profits in his second tax year of trading are:**

£ [ ]

**Overlap profits are:**

£ [ ]

## Task 3.3

Mr Mug ceased trading on 31 December 2014. His overlap profits brought forward amount to £9,000. His profits for the last few periods of account were:

|  | £ |
|---|---|
| Year ended 30 April 2012 | 36,000 |
| Year ended 30 April 2013 | 48,000 |
| Year ended 30 April 2014 | 16,000 |
| Eight months ended 31 December 2014 | 4,000 |

**Mr Mug's final tax year is** (insert as xxxx/xx)

[ ]

**Mr Mug's penultimate tax year is** (insert as xxxx/xx)

[ ]

**His taxable profits in his final tax year of trading are:**

£ [ ]

## Task 3.4

Jackie Smith started her picture framing business on 1 May 2010. Due to falling profits she ceased to trade on 28 February 2015.

Her profits for the whole period of trading were as follows.

|  | £ |
|---|---|
| 1 May 2010 – 31 July 2011 | 18,000 |
| 1 August 2011 – 31 July 2012 | 11,700 |
| 1 August 2012 – 31 July 2013 | 8,640 |
| 1 August 2013 – 31 July 2014 | 4,800 |
| 1 August 2014 – 28 February 2015 | 5,100 |

**Jackie's first tax year is** (insert as xxxx/xx)

[                    ]

**Her taxable profits in her first tax year of trading are:**

£ [                ]

**Jackie's second tax year is** (insert as xxxx/xx)

[                    ]

**Her taxable profits in her second tax year of trading are:**

£ [                ]

**Jackie's final tax year is** (insert as xxxx/xx)

[                    ]

**Her taxable profits in her final tax year of trading are:**

£ [                ]

**Over the life of her business Jackie is assessed on total profits of:**

£ [                ]

## Task 3.5

Fimbo and Florrie commenced in partnership on 1 January 2013. They produce accounts to 31 December each year and their profits have been as follows:

|  | Taxable profit £ |
|---|---|
| Year ended 31 December 2013 | 10,000 |
| Year ended 31 December 2014 | 20,000 |
| Year ended 31 December 2015 | 25,000 |

Until 31 December 2014 Fimbo took 60% of the profits after receiving a £5,000 salary. Florrie took the remaining 40% of profits.

On 1 January 2015, Fimbo and Florrie invite Pom to join the partnership. It is agreed that Fimbo's salary will increase to £6,500 and the profits will then be split equally between the three partners.

Using the proforma layout provided, show the division of profit for the three periods of account. Fill in all unshaded boxes. Insert a 0 (zero) if necessary.

|  | Total £ | Fimbo £ | Florrie £ | Pom £ |
|---|---|---|---|---|
| **12 months to 31 December 2013** |  |  |  |  |
| Salary |  |  |  |  |
| Share of profits |  |  |  |  |
| Total for year |  |  |  |  |
| **12 months to 31 December 2014** |  |  |  |  |
| Salary |  |  |  |  |
| Share of profits |  |  |  |  |
| Total for year |  |  |  |  |
| **12 months to 31 December 2015** |  |  |  |  |
| Salary |  |  |  |  |
| Share of profits |  |  |  |  |
| Total for year |  |  |  |  |

## Task 3.6

John, Paul and George began to trade as partners on 1 January 2012. The profits of the partnership are shared in the ratio 4:3:3. The accounts for recent periods have shown the following results:

|  | £ |
|---|---|
| Period to 31 July 2012 | 24,300 |
| Year to 31 July 2013 | 16,200 |
| Year to 31 July 2014 | 14,900 |

(1) Using the proforma layout provided, show the allocation of trading profits for all three periods of account. Fill in all unshaded boxes. Insert a 0 (zero) if necessary.

| | Total £ | John £ | Paul £ | George £ |
|---|---|---|---|---|
| **Period ended 31 July 2012** | | | | |
| Division of profits | | | | |
| **Year ended 31 July 2013** | | | | |
| Division of profits | | | | |
| **Year ended 31 July 2014** | | | | |
| Division of profits | | | | |

(2) Using the proforma layout provided, calculate the taxable trading profits of John, Paul and George for all tax years. Fill in all boxes.

| | John £ | Paul £ | George £ |
|---|---|---|---|
| 2011/12 | | | |
| 2012/13 | | | |
| 2013/14 | | | |
| 2014/15 | | | |

## Task 3.7

Strange and his partners Pavin and Lehman had traded for many years. Strange had contributed £20,000 to the business and Pavin £10,000.

Profits were shared in the ratio of 3:2:1 after providing Strange and Pavin with salaries of £15,000 and £5,000 and interest on capital of 5%.

On 1 August 2014 the profit sharing arrangements were changed to 2:2:1 after providing only Strange with a salary of £20,000, and no further interest on capital for any of the partners.

The partnership profit for the year to 31 December 2014 was £48,000.

**Using the proforma layout provided, show the allocation of profit for the year to 31 December 2014. Fill in all unshaded boxes. Insert a 0 (zero) if necessary.**

| | Total | Strange | Pavin | Lehman |
|---|---|---|---|---|
| **Year ended 31 December 2014** | £ | £ | £ | £ |
| **To 31 July 2014** | | | | |
| Salaries | | | | |
| Interest on capital | | | | |
| Division of profits | | | | |
| **To 31 December 2014** | | | | |
| Salary | | | | |
| Division of profits | | | | |
| Total for year ended 31 December 2014 | | | | |

## Task 3.8

Bob, Annie and John started their partnership on 1 June 2008 and make accounts up to 31 May each year. The accounts have always shown taxable profits.

For the period up to 31 January 2014 each partner received a salary of £15,000 per annum and the remaining profits were shared 50% to Bob and 25% each to Annie and John. There was no interest on capital.

Bob left the partnership on 1 February 2014. The profit sharing ratio, after the same salaries, changed to 50% each to Annie and John.

Profits for the year ending 31 May 2014 were £90,000.

**Using the proforma layout provided, calculate each partner's share of the profits for the year to 31 May 2014. Fill in all unshaded boxes. Insert a 0 (zero) if necessary.**

| | Total | Bob | Annie | John |
|---|---|---|---|---|
| **Year ended 31 May 2014** | £ | £ | £ | £ |
| **To 31 January 2014** | | | | |
| Salaries | | | | |
| Division of profits | | | | |
| **To 31 May 2014** | | | | |
| Salaries | | | | |
| Division of profits | | | | |
| Total for year ended 31 May 2014 | | | | |

# Task 3.9

**This style of task is human marked in the live assessment.**

Anne Curtis and Bettina Stone have been trading in partnership selling designer dresses for many years, making up accounts to 31 December each year. They share profits equally.

The following information relates to the year to 31 December 2014:

|  | £ |
|---|---|
| Revenue | 125,000 |
| Cost of goods bought | 75,000 |
| Rental of shop | 12,000 |
| General administration | 1,700 |
| Accountancy | 650 |
| Goods taken for own use (market value) | 1,550 |
| New sewing machine for alterations | 1,200 |

| The partnership received interest in the year to 5 April 2015 of: | |
|---|---|
| Gross bank interest received (including tax credit) | 8,000 |
| Tax deducted on bank interest | 1,600 |

**Using this information, complete page 6 of the Partnership Tax return which follows for Anne Curtis.**

## PARTNERSHIP STATEMENT (SHORT) *for the year ended 5 April 2015*

*Please read these instructions before completing the Statement*

Use these pages to allocate partnership income if the only income for the relevant return period was trading and professional income or taxed interest and alternative finance receipts from banks and building societies. Otherwise you must download or ask the SA Orderline for the *Partnership Statement (Full)* pages to record details of the allocation of all the partnership income. Go to hmrc.gov.uk/selfassessmentforms

*Step 1*   Fill in boxes 1 to 29 and boxes A and B as appropriate. Get the figures you need from the relevant boxes in the Partnership Tax Return. Complete a separate Statement for each accounting period covered by this Partnership Tax Return and for each trade or profession carried on by the partnership.

*Step 2*   Then allocate the amounts in boxes 11 to 29 attributable to each partner using the allocation columns on this page and page 7, read the Partnership Tax Return Guide, go to hmrc.gov.uk/selfassessmentforms If the partnership has more than three partners, please photocopy page 7.

*Step 3*   Each partner will need a copy of their allocation of income to fill in their personal tax return.

### PARTNERSHIP INFORMATION
If the partnership business includes a trade or profession, enter here the accounting period for which appropriate items in this statement are returned.

Start    **1**   /   /

End    **2**   /   /

Nature of trade    **3**

### MIXED PARTNERSHIPS

Tick here if this Statement is drawn up using Corporation Tax rules **4**

Tick here if this Statement is drawn up using tax rules for non-residents **5**

### Individual partner details

**6** Name of partner

Address

Postcode

Date appointed as a partner
(if during 2013–14 or 2014–15)
**7**   /   /

Partner's Unique Taxpayer Reference (UTR)
**8**

Date ceased to be a partner
(if during 2013–14 or 2014–15)
**9**   /   /

Partner's National Insurance number
**10**

### Partnership's profits, losses, income, tax credits, etc.

Tick this box if the items entered in the box had foreign tax taken off

### Partner's share of profits, losses, income, tax credits, etc.

Copy figures in boxes 11 to 29 to boxes in the individual's **Partnership (short)** pages as shown below

**• for an accounting period ended in 2014–15 ▼**

| | | | | | |
|---|---|---|---|---|---|
| from box 3.83 Profit from a trade or profession | **A** | **11** £ | Profit **11** £ | | Copy this figure to box 8 |
| from box 3.82 Adjustment on change of basis | | **11A** £ | **11A** £ | | Copy this figure to box 10 |
| from box 3.84 Loss from a trade or profession | **B** | **12** £ | Loss **12** £ | | Copy this figure to box 8 |
| from box 10.4 Business Premises Renovation Allowance | | **12A** £ | **12A** £ | | Copy this figure to box 15 |

**• for the period 6 April 2014 to 5 April 2015\***

| | | | | |
|---|---|---|---|---|
| from box 7.9A UK taxed interest and taxed alternative finance receipts | **22** £ | **22** £ | | Copy this figure to box 28 |
| from box 3.97 CIS deductions made by contractors on account of tax | **24** £ | **24** £ | | Copy this figure to box 30 |
| from box 3.98 Other tax taken off trading income | **24A** £ | **24A** £ | | Copy this figure to box 31 |
| from box 7.8A Income Tax taken off | **25** £ | **25** £ | | Copy this figure to box 29 |
| from box 3.117 Partnership charges | **29** £ | **29** £ | | Copy this figure to box 4, 'Other tax reliefs' section on page Ai 2 in your personal tax return |

*\* If you are a 'CT Partnership' see the Partnership Tax Return Guide*

SA800 2015      PARTNERSHIP TAX RETURN: PAGE 6

# Incorporated businesses

## Task 4.1

Righteous plc used to make its accounts up to 31 December. However, the directors decided to change the accounting date to 31 May and make up accounts for a 17-month period to 31 May 2015. The following information relates to the period of account from 1 January 2014 to 31 May 2015:

|  | £ |
|---|---|
| Trading profit | 500,000 |
| Property business income | 15,300 |
| Capital gain on property sold on: | |
| 1 May 2015 | 3,000 |
| Qualifying charitable donations paid on: | |
| 28 February 2014 | 15,000 |
| 31 August 2014 | 15,000 |
| 28 February 2015 | 40,000 |

No capital allowances are claimed.

**Using the proforma layout provided, compute taxable total profits for the accounting periods based on the above accounts. Use brackets for deductions and insert 0 (zero) if necessary, in order to fill in all unshaded boxes.**

|  | Year to 31 December 2014 | Five months to 31 May 2015 |
|---|---|---|
|  | £ | £ |
| Trading profits |  |  |
| Property business income |  |  |
| Chargeable gain |  |  |
| Total profits |  |  |
| Qualifying charitable donations paid |  |  |
| Taxable total profits |  |  |

# Task 4.2

When a company has a period of account which exceeds 12 months, how are the following apportioned:

| | Time apportioned | Period in which arises | Separate computation |
|---|---|---|---|
| Capital allowances | ☐ | ☐ | ☐ |
| Trading income | ☐ | ☐ | ☐ |
| Property income | ☐ | ☐ | ☐ |
| Interest income | ☐ | ☐ | ☐ |
| Chargeable gain | ☐ | ☐ | ☐ |

# Task 4.3

T Ltd has four wholly owned trading subsidiaries. It had taxable total profits for the eight months to 30 November 2014 of £38,000 and had franked investment income (gross dividends) of £4,000.

(1) **The upper limit for marginal relief for T Ltd will be:**

£ 

(2) **The lower limit for marginal relief for T Ltd will be:**

£ 

(3) **The corporation tax payable is:**

£ 

# Task 4.4

Rosemary Ltd has the following results for the ten-month period ended 31 March 2015:

| | £ |
|---|---|
| Taxable trading profits | 600,000 |
| Property business income | 300,000 |
| Dividends received | 162,000 |

(1)   **The augmented profits for Rosemary Ltd are:**

£ [          ]

(2)   **The upper limit for marginal relief for Rosemary Ltd will be:**

£ [          ]

(3)   **The lower limit for marginal relief for Rosemary Ltd will be:**

£ [          ]

(4)   **By filling in the boxes, compute the corporation tax payable.**

£

[          ] @ 21%                                        [       ]

Less:

1/400 × [          ] minus [          ] × [          ]      [       ]

Corporation Tax payable                                   [       ]

## Task 4.5

Island Ltd has two wholly owned trading subsidiaries. In order to align its accounts date with its subsidiaries, Island Ltd draws up accounts for the eight months to 31 December 2014, showing the following results.

|                    | £       |
|--------------------|---------|
| Trading profits    | 300,000 |
| Chargeable gain    | 60,000  |

(1)   **The taxable total profits for Island Ltd are:**

£ [          ]

(2)   **The upper limit for marginal relief for Island Ltd will be:**

£ [          ]

(3)   **The corporation tax payable is:**

£ [          ]

## Task 4.6

Basil Ltd, a company with no associated companies had the following results:

|  | 9 months to 30.6.14 £ |
|---|---|
| Trading profits | 1,000,000 |
| Chargeable gains | 120,000 |
| Dividend received (net) | 9,000 |

(1) **The augmented profits for Basil Ltd are:**

£ [ ]

(2) **The upper limit for marginal relief for Basil Ltd will be:**

£ [ ]

(3) **The corporation tax payable is:**

£ [ ]

..........................................................................................................

## Task 4.7

**This style of task is human marked in the live assessment.**

Cranmore Ltd is a trading company manufacturing specialist engineering tools. It makes up its accounts to 31 March each year. It has no associated companies.

For the year to 31 March 2015, the company had the following results:

|  | £ |
|---|---|
| Revenue | 525,000 |
| Trading profit before capital allowances | 405,000 |
| Interest received from building society deposit | 3,000 |
| Property business income from letting out part of factory | 16,000 |
|  | 424,000 |

The capital allowances have been computed to be £11,000, of which £3,000 is Annual Investment Allowance, £5,500 is writing down allowance on the main pool and £2,500 is writing down allowance on the special rate pool.

**Using the above information, show the entries that need to be made on the Form CT600.**

Page 2

# Company tax calculation

### Turnover

| 1 | Total turnover from trade or profession | **1** £ |
|---|---|---|

### Income

| 3 | Trading and professional profits | **3** £ |
|---|---|---|
| 4 | Trading losses brought forward claimed against profits | **4** £ |
| 5 | Net trading and professional profits | *box 3 minus box 4* <br> **5** £ |
| 6 | Bank, building society or other interest, and profits and gains from non-trading loan relationships | **6** £ |
| 11 | Income from UK land and buildings | **11** £ |
| 14 | Annual profits and gains not falling under any other heading | **14** £ |

### Chargeable gains

| 16 | Gross chargeable gains | **16** £ |
|---|---|---|
| 17 | Allowable losses including losses brought forward | **17** £ |
| 18 | Net chargeable gains | *box 16 minus box 17* <br> **18** £ |

| **21** | **Profits before other deductions and reliefs** | *sum of boxes 5, 6, 11, 14 & 18* <br> **21** £ |
|---|---|---|

### Deductions and Reliefs

| 24 | Management expenses under S75 ICTA 1988 | **24** £ |
|---|---|---|
| 30 | Trading losses of this or a later accounting period under S393A ICTA 1988 | **30** £ |
| 31 | Put an 'X' in box 31 if amounts carried back from later accounting periods are included in box 30 | **31** |
| 32 | Non-trade capital allowances | **32** £ |
| 35 | Charges paid | **35** £ |

| **37** | **Taxable total profits** | *box 21 minus boxes 24, 30, 32 and 35* <br> **37** £ |
|---|---|---|

### Tax calculation

| 38 | Franked investment income | **38** £ |
|---|---|---|
| 39 | Number of associated companies in this period <br> or | **39** |
| 40 | Associated companies in the first financial year | **40** |
| 41 | Associated companies in the second financial year | **41** |
| 42 | Put an 'X' in box 42 if the company claims to be charged at the starting rate or the small companies' rate on any part of its profits, or is claiming marginal rate relief | **42** |

Enter how much profit has to be charged and at what rate of tax

| Financial year (yyyy) | Amount of profit | Rate of tax | Tax | |
|---|---|---|---|---|
| **43** | **44** £ | **45** | **46** £ | p |
| **53** | **54** £ | **55** | **56** £ | p |
| | | | *total of boxes 46 and 56* | |
| 63 Corporation tax | | | **63** £ | p |

| 64 | Marginal rate relief | **64** £ | p |
|---|---|---|---|
| 65 | Corporation tax net of marginal rate relief | **65** £ | p |
| 66 | Underlying rate of corporation tax | **66** • % | |
| 67 | Profits matched with non-corporate distributions | **67** | |
| 68 | Tax at non-corporate distributions rate | **68** £ | p |
| 69 | Tax at underlying rate on remaining profits | **69** £ | p |
| **70** | **Corporation tax chargeable** | *See note for box 70 in CT600 Guide* <br> **70** £ | p |

CT600 (Short) (2008) Version 2

# Losses

## Task 5.1

Pipchin has traded for many years, making up accounts to 30 September each year. His recent results have been:

| Year ended | £ |
|---|---|
| 30 September 2012 | 12,000 |
| 30 September 2013 | (45,000) |
| 30 September 2014 | 8,000 |
| 30 September 2015 | 14,000 |

He has received property income as follows:

| | £ |
|---|---|
| 2012/13 | 10,400 |
| 2013/14 | 11,000 |
| 2014/15 | 11,000 |
| 2015/16 | 11,000 |

**Using the proforma layout provided, compute Pipchin's net income for 2012/13 to 2014/16, assuming maximum claims for loss relief are made as early as possible. If an answer is zero, insert 0, and show the offset of losses within brackets. Fill in all boxes.**

| | 2012/13 | 2013/14 | 2014/15 | 2015/16 |
|---|---|---|---|---|
| | £ | £ | £ | £ |
| Trading profits | | | | |
| Trading loss offset against future year | | | | |
| Property income | | | | |
| Trading loss offset against current year | | | | |
| Trading loss offset against previous year | | | | |
| Net income | | | | |

## Task 5.2

**Identify whether the following statement is True or False.**

An individual can restrict a claim to set a trading loss against total income in order to have enough net income to use his personal allowance.

| | ✓ |
|---|---|
| True | |
| False | |

....................................................................................................

## Task 5.3

**Identify whether the following statement is True or False.**

An individual must make a trading loss claim against total income in the tax year of the loss before making a claim to set the loss against total income in the preceding year.

| | ✓ |
|---|---|
| True | |
| False | |

....................................................................................................

## Task 5.4

**Identify whether the following statement is True or False.**

An individual can only carry a trading loss forward against trading income of the same trade.

| | ✓ |
|---|---|
| True | |
| False | |

....................................................................................................

## Task 5.5

Pennington Ltd produced the following results:

| | Year ended 30 June | | |
|---|---|---|---|
| | 2012 | 2013 | 2014 |
| | £ | £ | £ |
| Trading profit/(loss) | 62,000 | 20,000 | (83,000) |
| Interest income | 1,200 | 600 | 1,200 |
| Qualifying charitable donation | 100 | 50 | 100 |

(1) **Using the proforma layout provided, compute Pennington Ltd's taxable total profits for the above accounting periods, assuming the loss relief is claimed as soon as possible. Fill in all boxes. Use brackets for loss relief and add a 0 (zero) where necessary.**

| | Year ended 30 June | | |
|---|---|---|---|
| | 2012 | 2013 | 2014 |
| Trading profits | | | |
| Interest | | | |
| Total profits | | | |
| Current period loss relief | | | |
| Carry back loss relief | | | |
| Total profits after loss relief | | | |
| Qualifying charitable donation | | | |
| Taxable total profits | | | |

(2) **The trading loss available to carry forward at 30 June 2014 is:**

£ [        ]

· · · · · · · · · · · · · · · · · · · · · · · · · · · · · · · · · · · · · · · · · · · · · · · · · · · · · · · · · · · · · · · · · · · · · · · · · · · · · · · · · · ·

# Task 5.6

Ferraro Ltd has the following results.

| | Year ended 30.9.12 £ | 9 months to 30.6.13 £ | Year ended 30.6.14 £ | Year ended 30.6.15 £ |
|---|---|---|---|---|
| Trading profit (loss) | 6,200 | 4,320 | (100,000) | 53,000 |
| Bank deposit interest accrued | 80 | 240 | 260 | 200 |
| Rents receivable | 1,420 | 1,440 | 1,600 | 1,500 |
| Chargeable gain | – | 12,680 | – | – |
| Allowable capital loss | (5,000) | – | (9,423) | – |
| Qualifying charitable donation | 1,000 | 1,000 | 1,500 | 1,500 |

(1) **Using the proforma layout provided, compute all taxable total profits, claiming loss reliefs as early as possible. Fill in all boxes. Use brackets for loss relief and add a 0 (zero) where necessary.**

|  | Year ended 30.9.12 | 9 months to 30.6.13 | Year ended 30.6.14 | Year ended 30.6.15 |
|---|---|---|---|---|
| Trading profits |  |  |  |  |
| Carry forward loss relief |  |  |  |  |
| Interest |  |  |  |  |
| Property income |  |  |  |  |
| Chargeable gains |  |  |  |  |
| Total profits |  |  |  |  |
| Current period loss relief |  |  |  |  |
| Carry back loss relief |  |  |  |  |
| Total profits after loss relief |  |  |  |  |
| Qualifying charitable donation |  |  |  |  |
| Taxable total profits |  |  |  |  |

(2) **The trading loss available to carry forward at 30 June 2015 is:**

£ 

(3) **The capital loss available to carry forward at 30 June 2015 is:**

£ 

**Task 5.7**

**Identify whether the following statement is True or False.**

A company must offset its trading loss against total profits in the loss-making period before carrying the loss back.

|  | ✓ |
|---|---|
| True |  |
| False |  |

## Task 5.8

**Identify whether the following statement is True or False.**

If a company carries a trading loss forward, the loss can be set against total profits in the following accounting period.

| | ✓ |
|---|---|
| True | |
| False | |

## Task 5.9

**Identify whether the following statement is True or False.**

A company can set-off a capital loss against trading profits.

| | ✓ |
|---|---|
| True | |
| False | |

# National insurance

## Task 6.1

Abraham has trading profits of £12,830 for the year ended 31 December 2014.

**The Class 2 NIC liability for 2014/15 is:**

| £ | | . | |
|---|---|---|---|

**The Class 4 NIC liability for 2014/15 is:**

| £ | | . | |
|---|---|---|---|

**The total NIC liability for 2014/15 is:**

| £ | | . | |
|---|---|---|---|

## Task 6.2

John has profits of £48,000 for the year ended 31 March 2015.

**The Class 2 NIC liability for 2014/15 is:**

| £ | | . | |
|---|---|---|---|

**The Class 4 NIC liability for 2014/15 is:**

| £ | | . | |
|---|---|---|---|

**The total NIC liability for 2014/15 is:**

| £ | | . | |
|---|---|---|---|

## Task 6.3

Raj has accounting profits of £4,000 and trading profits of £3,500 for 2014/15.

**The Class 2 NIC liability for 2014/15 is:**

| £ | | . | |
|---|---|---|---|

**The Class 4 NIC liability for 2014/15 is:**

| £ | | . | |
|---|---|---|---|

The total NIC liability for 2014/15 is:

| £ | | • | |
|---|---|---|---|

........................................................................

## Task 6.4

Zoë is a self employed author who starts in business on 6 April 2014. In the year to 5 April 2015 she had taxable trading profits of £80,000.

(1)   The date by which Zoe must notify that she is liable to Class 2 NICs is: (insert the date as xx/xx/xxxx)

| |
|---|
| |

(2)   **The Class 2 NIC liability for 2014/15 is:**

| £ | | • | |
|---|---|---|---|

**The Class 4 NIC liability for 2014/15 is:**

| £ | | • | |
|---|---|---|---|

**The total NIC liability for 2014/15 is:**

| £ | | • | |
|---|---|---|---|

........................................................................

## Task 6.5

Wendy and Jayne have been in partnership as interior designers for many years, trading as Dramatic Decors.

On 1 January 2015, Wendy and Jayne admitted Paula to the partnership. From that date, partnership profits were shared 40% to each of Wendy and Jayne and 20% to Paula. The partnership continued to make up its accounts to 31 December and the trading profit for the year to 31 December 2015 was £160,000.

Paula had not worked for many years prior to becoming a partner in Dramatic Decors.

(1)   **The share of profits taxable on Paula for 2014/15 is:**

| £ | |
|---|---|

**and for 2015/16 is:**

| £ | |
|---|---|

**and the overlap profits to carry forward are:**

£ _____

(2) **The Class 4 National Insurance Contributions payable by Paula for 2014/15 are:**

£ _____ **.** _____

# Tax administration

## Task 7.1

Identify by which date an Individual should normally submit his 2014/15 self-assessment tax return if it is to be filed online. Tick ONE box.

|  | ✓ |
|---|---|
| 31 January 2016 |  |
| 5 April 2016 |  |
| 31 October 2015 |  |
| 31 December 2015 |  |

## Task 7.2

Gordon had income tax payable of £14,500 in 2013/14. His income tax payable for 2014/15 was £20,500.

**How will Gordon settle his income tax payable for 2014/15? Tick ONE box.**

|  | ✓ |
|---|---|
| The full amount of £20,500 will be paid on 31 January 2016. |  |
| Payments on account based on the estimated 2014/15 liability will be made on 31 January and 31 July 2015, with the balance payable on 31 January 2016. |  |
| Payments on account of £10,250 will be made on 31 January and 31 July 2015 with nothing due on 31 January 2016. |  |
| Payments on account of £7,250 will be made on 31 January and 31 July 2015, with the balance of £6,000 being paid on 31 January 2016. |  |

## Task 7.3

The minimum penalty as a percentage of Potential Lost Revenue for a deliberate and concealed error on a tax return where there is a prompted disclosure is:

|  | ✓ |
|---|---|
| 100% |  |
| 50% |  |
| 35% |  |
| 15% |  |

## Task 7.4

**The maximum penalty as a percentage of Potential Lost Revenue for careless error for failure to notify chargeability is:**

| | ✓ |
|---|---|
| 0% | |
| 20% | |
| 30% | |
| 35% | |

## Task 7.5

**Identify whether the following statement is True or False.**

If an individual files her 2014/15 return online on 13 April 2016, the penalty for late filing is £100.

| | ✓ |
|---|---|
| True | |
| False | |

## Task 7.6

**Identify whether the following statement is True or False.**

The penalty for failure to keep records is £3,000 per tax year or accounting period.

| | ✓ |
|---|---|
| True | |
| False | |

## Task 7.7

**Identify whether the following statement is True or False.**

An individual is required to make a payment on account on 31 July 2015 for 2014/15. The payment is actually made on 10 November 2015.

The penalty payable is 5%.

| | ✓ |
|---|---|
| True | |
| False | |

························································································

## Task 7.8

Boscobel plc has paid corporation tax at the main rate for many years. For the year ending 31 March 2015, it had a corporation tax liability of £500,000.

**Fill in the table below showing how it will pay its corporation tax liability.**

| Instalment | Due date (xx/xx/xxxx) | Amount due (£) |
|---|---|---|
| 1 | | |
| 2 | | |
| 3 | | |
| 4 | | |

························································································

## Task 7.9

**Tick whether the following statements are True or False.**

| | True | False |
|---|---|---|
| A company with a period of account ending on 31 March 2015 must keep its records until 31 March 2017. | ☐ | ☐ |
| The due date for payment of CGT for 2014/15 is 31 January 2016. | ☐ | ☐ |
| An individual who becomes chargeable to income tax in 2014/15 must notify HMRC by 31 October 2015. | ☐ | ☐ |
| A large company will not have to pay corporation tax by instalments if it has augmented profits not exceeding £10m and was not large in the previous accounting period. | ☐ | ☐ |
| A company which pays corporation tax at the small profits rate must pay its corporation tax by nine months and one day after the end of its accounting period. | ☐ | ☐ |

························································································

## Chargeable gains – the basics

### Task 8.1

**Complete the following sentence by filling in the gaps:**

For the gain on the disposal of a capital asset to be a chargeable gain there must be a chargeable [           ] of a chargeable [           ] by a chargeable [           ].

......................................................................................

### Task 8.2

**Identify whether the following assets are chargeable assets or exempt assets for CGT:**

| Item | Chargeable | Exempt |
|---|---|---|
| Wasting chattel with useful life of 25 years | ☐ | ☐ |
| Disposal of half the holding of a plot of land | ☐ | ☐ |
| Car used for business purposes | ☐ | ☐ |

......................................................................................

### Task 8.3

Romana purchased a freehold holiday cottage for £40,000. She then spent £5,000 on a new conservatory. She sold the cottage for £90,000 on 15 March 2015. Romana had not made any other disposals during 2014/15.

**What is her taxable gain for 2014/15?**

|  | ✓ |
|---|---|
| £34,000 | |
| £39,000 | |
| £45,000 | |
| £50,000 | |

......................................................................................

## Task 8.4

In August 2014 George made chargeable gains of £20,000 and allowable losses of £3,560. He made no other disposals during 2014/15 and he is a higher rate taxpayer.

(1) **George's capital gains tax liability for 2014/15 is:**

£ [                    ]

(2) **George's capital gains tax liability is payable by:**

[                    ]

---

## Task 8.5

In November 2014, Graham made chargeable gains of £15,000 and allowable losses of £5,200. He made no other disposals during 2014/15.

**The amount of the loss Graham will use in 2014/15 is:**

£ [                ]

---

## Task 8.6

Gayle made chargeable gains of £5,000 in August 2014 and £17,500 in November 2014. In July 2014 she made allowable losses of £2,000. She has unused basic rate band of £5,000 in 2014/15.

**Gayle's capital gains tax liability for 2014/15 is:**

£ [                ]

---

## Task 8.7

Gerry made chargeable gains of £27,000 in December 2014. She made no other disposals in the year. Her taxable income (ie after deducting the personal allowance) for 2014/15 was £22,910. Note the limit for the basic rate band for 2014/15 is £31,865.

**Gerry's capital gains tax liability for 2014/15 is:**

£ [                ]

---

## Task 8.8

Kevin made gains of £17,800 and losses of £6,600 in 2014/15. He has losses brought forward of £5,000.

**The losses to carry forward to 2015/16 are:**

| £ | |
|---|---|

## Task 8.9

Elias has the following gains and losses arising from disposals of chargeable assets:

| Tax year | 2012/13 | 2013/14 | 2014/15 |
|---|---|---|---|
| Gains | £2,000 | £4,000 | £13,700 |
| Losses | £(14,000) | £(2,000) | £(2,000) |

**The maximum allowable loss carried forward to 2015/16 will be:**

| £ | |
|---|---|

## Task 8.10

On 14 April 2014, Fire Ltd sold a factory for £230,000. This had originally been purchased in April 1993 for £140,000.

**Assumed Indexation factor**

April 1993 – April 2014      0.819

**Using the proforma layout provided calculate the chargeable gain arising on the disposal of the factory. Fill in all boxes. Add a 0 (zero) if necessary.**

| | £ |
|---|---|
| Proceeds | |
| Less cost | |
| Unindexed gain | |
| Less indexation allowance | |
| Chargeable gain/allowable loss | |

## Task 8.11

On 18 July 2014, Earth plc sold a warehouse for £180,000. This had been purchased in May 2004 for £100,000. Earth plc had spent £25,000 on an extension to the warehouse in August 2006.

**Assumed Indexation factors**

May 2004 – July 2014      0.375
May 2004 – August 2006    0.068
August 2006 – July 2014   0.287

**Using the proforma layout provided calculate the chargeable gain arising on the disposal of the warehouse. Fill in all boxes. Add a 0 (zero) if necessary.**

|  | £ |
|---|---|
| Proceeds | |
| Less   cost | |
|         enhancement expenditure | |
| Unindexed gain | |
| Less   indexation allowance on cost | |
|         indexation allowance on enhancement | |
| Chargeable gain | |

## Task 8.12

**Identify whether the following statement is True or False.**

A company is entitled to an annual exempt amount.

|  | ✓ |
|---|---|
| True | |
| False | |

# Further aspects of chargeable gains

## Task 9.1

Harry bought a three-acre plot of land for £150,000. He sold two acres of the land at auction for £240,000. His disposal costs were £3,000. The market value of the one remaining acre at the date of sale was £60,000.

(1)  **The cost of the land sold is:**

£ 

(2)  **The gain on sale is:**

£ 

## Task 9.2

Leonora purchased a picture for £5,500 and sold it in September 2014 for £7,500, incurring £300 expenses of sale.

**Her chargeable gain on sale is:**

|        | ✓ |
|--------|---|
| £2,300 |   |
| £2,000 |   |
| £2,500 |   |
| £1,700 |   |

## Task 9.3

Mark purchased an antique vase for £9,000. He sold the vase in August 2014 at auction for £4,500 net of auctioneer's fees of 10%.

**Mark's allowable loss is:**

£ 

## Task 9.4

**Identify whether the following statement is True or False.**

Chloe bought a necklace for £4,000. She sold it in September 2014 for £5,500.

Chloe has a chargeable gain on sale of £1,500.

| | ✓ |
|---|---|
| True | |
| False | |

## Task 9.5

In August 2014, John gave his daughter an asset worth £10,000. He had acquired the asset for £25,000.

In March 2015, John gave his brother an asset worth £60,000. John had acquired the asset for £15,000.

**John's chargeable gains (before the annual exempt amount) for 2014/15 are:**

| | ✓ |
|---|---|
| £45,000 | |
| £30,000 | |
| £34,100 | |
| £19,100 | |

## Task 9.6

**Identify whether the following statement is True or False.**

A disposal to a connected person is at market value.

| | ✓ |
|---|---|
| True | |
| False | |

## Task 9.7

On 14 November 2014, Wind plc sold two offices for £140,000. These had been part of a large office block. The whole block had cost £250,000 in August 2001 and in November 2014 the remaining offices had a market value of £320,000.

**Indexation factor:**

August 2001 – November 2014      0.488

(1)  **The cost of the two offices disposed of is:**

£ ☐

(2)  **The chargeable gain arising on the disposal is:**

£ ☐

## Task 9.8

LM plc bought a painting in October 2006 for £4,500. It sold the painting at auction in September 2014 and received £7,500 after deducting the auctioneers' commission of £500. The indexation factor between October 2006 and September 2014 is 0.291

**Complete the following computation.**

|                                    | £ |
|------------------------------------|---|
| Proceeds                           | ☐ |
| Disposal costs                     | ☐ |
| Cost of acquisition                | ☐ |
| Indexation allowance               | ☐ |
| Gain                               | ☐ |
| Gain using chattel marginal relief | ☐ |
| Chargeable gain                    | ☐ |

# Shares

## Task 10.1

Jake sold 5,000 ordinary shares for £20,000 in JKL plc on 10 August 2014. He bought 6,000 shares in JKL plc for £9,000 on 15 July 2012 and another 1,000 shares for £4,200 on 16 August 2014.

**His net gain on sale is:**

| £ | |
|---|---|

## Task 10.2

Susan's dealings in K plc were as follows:

| | No of shares | Cost/(proceeds) £ |
|---|---|---|
| 10 February 1999 | 12,000 | 18,000 |
| 20 September 2006 | Bonus issue of 1 for 4 | Nil |
| 15 March 2015 | (2,000) | (8,000) |

**Using the proforma layout provided, calculate the gain on sale. Fill in all unshaded boxes. Use a 0 (zero) if necessary.**

*Share pool*

| | No of shares | Cost £ |
|---|---|---|
| 10 February 1999 | | |
| 20 September 2006 Bonus 1:4 | | |
| Total before disposal | | |
| 15 March 2015 Disposal | | |
| c/f | | |

*Gain on sale*

| | £ |
|---|---|
| Proceeds | |
| Less cost | |
| Gain | |

# Task 10.3

**This style of task is human marked in the live assessment.**

Geoff sold 10,000 of his shares in AC plc on 4 November 2014 for £60,000. The shares had been acquired as follows:

|  | No. of shares | Cost £ |
|---|---|---|
| 9 December 1999 | 12,000 | 4,400 |
| 12 October 2003 (rights issue 1:3 at £5) |  |  |
| 10 November 2014 | 2,000 | 11,500 |

**Compute the gain or loss made on these shares. Clearly show the balance of shares and their value to carry forward.**

|  |  |  |
|---|---|---|
|  |  |  |
|  |  |  |
|  |  |  |
|  |  |  |
|  |  |  |
|  |  |  |
|  |  |  |
|  |  |  |
|  |  |  |
|  |  |  |
|  |  |  |
|  |  |  |
|  |  |  |
|  |  |  |
|  |  |  |
|  |  |  |
|  |  |  |

## Task 10.4

**This style of task is human marked in the live assessment.**

Standring Ltd owned 20,000 shares in Smart plc acquired as follows:

5,000 shares acquired September 1993 for £10,000.

1 for 5 rights acquired October 2003 at £5 per share.

14,000 shares acquired August 2004 for £84,000.

Standring Ltd sold 18,000 shares in January 2015 for £155,000.

### Indexation factors

| | |
|---|---|
| September 1993 – October 2003 | 0.287 |
| October 2003 – August 2004 | 0.026 |
| August 2004 – January 2015 | 0.384 |

**Using the proforma layout provided, calculate the chargeable gain arising on the sale in January 2015.**

*FA 1985 pool*

| | | | |
|---|---|---|---|
| | | | |
| | | | |
| | | | |
| | | | |
| | | | |
| | | | |
| | | | |
| | | | |
| | | | |
| | | | |
| | | | |
| | | | |
| | | | |
| | | | |
| | | | |
| | | | |
| | | | |

*Gain*

| | |
|---|---|
| | |
| | |
| | |
| | |
| | |
| | |

----------------------------------------------------------------

## Task 10.5

**This style of task is human marked in the live assessment.**

Box plc sold 11,000 shares in Crate Ltd for £78,200 on 25 May 2014. These shares had been acquired as follows.

| 26 May 1995 | Purchased | 4,000 shares for | £24,000 |
| 30 June 1996 | 1 for 2 bonus issue | | |
| 24 October 2003 | Purchased | 5,000 shares for | £27,500 |

**Indexation factors**

| | |
|---|---|
| May 1995 – October 2003 | 0.221 |
| May 1995 – June 1996 | 0.023 |
| June 1996 – October 2003 | 0.193 |
| October 2003 – May 2014 | 0.401 |

**Using the proforma layout provided, calculate the gain on disposal.**

*FA 1985 pool*

| | | | |
|---|---|---|---|
| | | | |
| | | | |
| | | | |
| | | | |
| | | | |
| | | | |
| | | | |

| | | | |
|---|---|---|---|
| | | | |
| | | | |
| | | | |

*Gain*

| | |
|---|---|
| | |
| | |
| | |
| | |
| | |
| | |

........................................................................................

## Task 10.6

**Identify whether the following statement is True or False.**

Indexation allowance on rights issue shares runs from the date of the rights issue even though the rights issue shares are treated as having been acquired at the time of the original acquisition to which they relate.

| | ✔ |
|---|---|
| True | |
| False | |

........................................................................................

# Reliefs for gains

## Task 11.1

Ronald started in business as a sole trader in August 2006. He acquired a freehold shop for £80,000 and a warehouse for £150,000.

He sold his business as a going concern to Lesley in December 2014 and received £50,000 for goodwill, £90,000 for the shop and £130,000 for the warehouse. Ronald made no other chargeable gains in 2014/15 and he is a higher rate taxpayer.

**Using the proforma layout provided, compute the CGT payable by Ronald for 2014/15. Fill in all unshaded boxes. Use a 0 (zero) if necessary.**

|  | £ | £ |
|---|---|---|
| Proceeds of goodwill |  |  |
| Less cost |  |  |
| Gain/(loss) on goodwill |  |  |
| Proceeds of shop |  |  |
| Less cost |  |  |
| Gain/(loss) on shop |  |  |
| Proceeds of warehouse |  |  |
| Less cost |  |  |
| Gain/(loss) on warehouse |  |  |
| Net gains eligible for entrepreneurs' relief |  |  |
| Less annual exempt amount |  |  |
| Taxable gains |  |  |
| CGT payable |  |  |

## Task 11.2

**Identify whether the following statement is True or False.**

The lifetime limit of gains eligible for entrepreneurs' relief is £10,000,000.

|  | ✓ |
|---|---|
| True |  |
| False |  |

## Task 11.3

Simon acquired 10,000 Blue Ltd shares worth £65,000 in September 1991 as a gift from his father. The father had originally acquired them as an investment in 1986 and gift relief was claimed on the gain of £15,000. Simon sold the Blue Ltd shares for £200,000 on 30 November 2014. He has no other assets for CGT purposes and made no other disposals in 2014/15.

**The taxable gain arising on the sale of the Blue Ltd shares is:**

£ 

## Task 11.4

Fran gave a factory worth £500,000 to her friend Anna on 1 June 2014 and a claim for gift relief was made. Fran had bought the factory on 1 January 1996 for £75,000. On 1 July 2015 Anna sold the factory for £520,000.

(1) **Fran's chargeable gain on her disposal is:**

£ 

(2) **Anna's chargeable gain on her disposal is:**

£ 

## Task 11.5

On 6 April 1988 Edward acquired for £60,000 a small workshop where he carried on his trade as a furniture maker. On 6 August 2014 he sold the workshop for £125,000 having moved on 10 April 2014 to smaller premises which cost £123,500.

(1) **Edward's gain on the disposal before rollover relief is:**

£

(2)  **Assuming rollover relief is claimed, the gain immediately chargeable is:**

£ [            ]

(3)  **The gain which Edward can rollover into the new premises is:**

£ [            ]

## Task 11.6

On 23 May 2011 Del Ltd sold a freehold property for £145,000 which had cost originally £50,000 on 9 May 1998. On 15 April 2014 Del Ltd acquired the freehold of another property for £140,000. Rollover relief was claimed.

**Indexation factor**

May 1998 – May 2011    0.439

(1)  **The gain on disposal in May 2011 was:**

£ [            ]

(2)  **The gain available for rollover relief is:**

£ [            ]

(3)  **The base cost of the property acquired in April 2014 is:**

£ [            ]

## Task 11.7

L plc sold a plot of land.

**Tick the box that correctly finishes the following statement.**

If L plc wishes to claim rollover relief it must acquire a new asset between:

|  | ✓ |
| --- | --- |
| The start of the previous accounting period and the end of the next accounting period | |
| Three years before and three years after the date of the disposal | |
| One year before and three years after the date of the disposal | |
| One year before and one year after the date of the disposal | |

# Answer bank

**Answer bank**

# Business Tax – Practice tasks answers

## Adjustment to profits

### Task 1.1

| From: | AAT student |
|---|---|
| To: | A Client |
| Date: | 14 June 2015 |
| Subject: | Badges of trade |

In order to decide whether a trade is being carried on the following 'badges of trade' need to be considered:

(a) *Subject matter.* When people engage in trade, they frequently do so by purchasing and re-selling objects with a view to making a profit. Objects bought for this purpose are often not the type of objects that would be bought for investment or enjoyment. This means that the subject matter of a transaction will very often indicate whether a trade is being carried on or not.

(b) *Length of ownership.* A short period of ownership is an indication of an intention to trade in a commodity.

(c) *Frequency of transactions.* Where the same type of article is repeatedly bought and sold, it will normally suggest that there is trading in that article.

(d) *Supplementary work* on or in connection with the property sold, eg modification, processing, packaging, or renovating the item sold suggests the carrying on of a trade.

(e) *Acquisition of asset.* If goods are acquired deliberately, trading may be indicated. If goods are acquired by gift or inheritance, their later sale is unlikely to constitute trading.

(f) *Profit motive.* This is usually the most important consideration though its absence does not prevent a trade being carried on if, in fact, the operation is run on commercial lines and a profit does result.

These *badges of trade* are only general indications and, in each case, all the facts must be considered before any decision can be made.

## Task 1.2

| | £ | £ |
|---|---|---|
| Profit for the year per accounts | | 5,300 |
| | Add | Deduct |
| staff wages | 0 | 0 |
| Mr Jelly's salary (N1) | 260 | 0 |
| light and heat | 0 | 0 |
| motor expenses (N2) (£350 × 1/7) | 50 | 0 |
| postage, stationery and telephone | 0 | 0 |
| painting shop internally | 0 | 0 |
| plant repairs | 0 | 0 |
| stockroom extension (N3) | 101 | 0 |
| Irrecoverable debts – provision (N4) | 200 | 0 |
| donations (N2) | 10 | 0 |
| advertising | 0 | 0 |
| entertaining (N5) | 90 | 0 |
| gifts (N6) | 70 | 0 |
| legal expenses | 0 | 0 |
| depreciation charge | 600 | 0 |
| Total net adjustments | | 1,381 |
| Taxable trading profit | | 6,681 |

**Notes**

(1) Appropriation of profit.
(2) Not expenditure incurred wholly and exclusively for the purpose of trade.
(3) Capital items.
(4) Increase in general provision is disallowed.
(5) Entertaining expenses specifically disallowed.
(6) Gifts of alcohol specifically disallowed.

## Task 1.3

| | Allow ✓ | Disallow and add back ✓ | Not taxable so deduct ✓ |
|---|---|---|---|
| Increase in specific provision | ✓ | | |
| Decrease in general provision | | | ✓ |
| Depreciation charge | | ✓ | |
| Cocktail party held for customers | | ✓ | |
| Political donation | | ✓ | |
| Employees salary | ✓ | | |
| Repair to factory roof | ✓ | | |

## Task 1.4

| | |
|---|---|
| Box 17 | £25000.00 |
| Box 21 | £1760.00 |
| Box 23 | £1700.00 |
| Box 26 | £150.00 |
| Box 28 | £1650.00 |
| Box 31 | £30260.00 |
| Box 43 | £500.00 |
| Box 46 | £500.00 |

## Task 1.5

| | £ | £ |
|---|---|---|
| Profit per accounts | | 656,980 |
| | Add | Deduct |
| depreciation charge | 83,420 | 0 |
| qualifying charitable donation | 1,900 | 0 |
| donation to local charity | 0 | 0 |
| gifts to customers | 900 | 0 |
| accountancy and audit fee | 0 | 0 |
| legal fees – renewal of 20 year lease | 0 | 0 |
| legal fees – issue of debenture | 0 | 0 |
| repairs – knocked down wall | 0 | 0 |
| initial repairs to office | 12,200 | 0 |
| other expenses | 0 | 0 |
| debenture interest | 0 | (24,700) |
| bank interest | 0 | (4,800) |
| dividends | 0 | (56,000) |
| capital allowances | 0 | (13,200) |
| interest payable on trading loans | 0 | 0 |
| Net adjustments | | (280) |
| Taxable trading profit | | 656,700 |

**Notes**

(1) The costs of renewing a short lease and of obtaining loan finance for trading purposes are allowable.

(2) The replacement of the wall is allowable since the whole structure is not being replaced. The repairs to the office building are not allowable, being capital in nature, as the building was not in a usable state when purchased and this was reflected in the purchase price.

# Task 1.6

| | Allow ✓ | Disallow and add back ✓ | Not taxable as trading income so deduct ✓ |
|---|---|---|---|
| Dividends received from an unconnected company | | | ✓ |
| Profit on sale of shares | | | ✓ |
| Running costs of car with 20% private use by an employee | ✓ | | |
| Parking fine of director | | ✓ | |
| Capital allowances | ✓ | | |
| Director's salary | ✓ | | |
| Bank interest received | | | ✓ |

# Capital allowances

## Task 2.1

|  | Revenue | Capital |
|---|---|---|
| Purchase of machinery |  | ✓ |
| Rent paid for premises | ✓ |  |
| Insurance of premises | ✓ |  |
| Repairs to roof of factory | ✓ |  |
| New extension to shop |  | ✓ |
| Purchase of new car for owner |  | ✓ |
| Legal fees relating to purchase of new factory |  | ✓ |
| Payment of staff wages | ✓ |  |
| Accountancy costs | ✓ |  |
| Redecoration of shop | ✓ |  |

# Task 2.2

| Y/e 5 April 2015 | AIA £ | Main pool £ | Mercedes car (80%) £ | Allowances £ |
|---|---|---|---|---|
| b/f | | 38,500 | | |
| AIA additions | | | | |
| 14.7.14 Furniture | 23,800 | | | |
| 2.4.15 Machinery | 31,000 | | | |
| | 54,800 | | | |
| AIA | (54,800) | | | 54,800 |
| Non-AIA additions | | | | |
| 30.3.15 Car | | | 18,000 | |
| 31.3.15 Car | | 8,000 | | |
| Disposals | | | | |
| 29.3.15 Machinery | | (3,000) | | |
| | | 43,500 | | |
| WDA @ 18% | | (7,830) | | 7,830 |
| WDA @ 18% | | | (3,240) × 80% | 2,592 |
| c/f | | 35,670 | 14,760 | |
| Allowances | | | | 65,222 |

## Task 2.3

| | AIA | FYA @ 100% | Main pool | Allowances |
|---|---|---|---|---|
| | £ | £ | £ | £ |
| *Y/e 31 December 2014* | | | | |
| *AIA addition* | | | | |
| 6.5.14 Machinery | 455,750 | | | |
| AIA (max) (W) | (437,500) | | | 437,500 |
| | 18,250 | | | |
| Transfer to main pool | (18,250) | | 18,250 | |
| | | | | |
| *FYA @ 100%* | | | | |
| 6.7.14 Low emission car | | 8,000 | | |
| FYA @ 100% | | (8,000) | | 8,000 |
| *Non-AIA addition* | | – | | |
| 31.08.14 Car | | | 10,500 | |
| | | | 28,750 | |
| WDA @ 18% | | | (5,175) | 5,175 |
| | | | | |
| c/f | | | 23,575 | |
| Total allowances | | | | 450,675 |

(w) Maximum AIA for y/e 31 December 2014

(£250,000 × 3/12 = £62,500) **plus** (£500,000 × 9/12 = £375,000) = £437,500

## Task 2.4

|  | Main pool | Car (1) @ 70% | Special rate pool | Car (2) @ 70% | Allowances |
|---|---|---|---|---|---|
|  | £ | £ | £ | £ | £ |
| Y/e 31 March 2015 |  |  |  |  |  |
| b/f | 120,000 | 21,000 | 17,500 |  |  |
| Non-AIA FYA/addition |  |  |  |  |  |
| 10.8.14 Car |  |  |  | 25,000 |  |
| Disposal |  |  |  |  |  |
| 10.8.14 Car |  | (16,000) |  |  |  |
| Balancing allowance |  | 5,000 × 70% |  |  | 3,500 |
| WDA @ 18% | (21,600) |  |  |  | 21,600 |
| WDA @ 8% |  |  | (1,400) |  | 1,400 |
| WDA @ 8% |  |  |  | (2,000) × 70% | 1,400 |
| c/f | 98,400 |  | 16,100 | 23,000 |  |
| Allowances |  |  |  |  | 27,900 |

## Task 2.5

|  | Main pool | Special rate pool | Allowances |
|---|---|---|---|
|  | £ | £ | £ |
| Y/e 31 March 2015 |  |  |  |
| b/f | 106,000 |  |  |
| Addition |  | 14,000 |  |
| WDA @ 18% | (19,080) |  | 19,080 |
| WDA @ 8% |  | (1,120) | 1,120 |
| c/f | 86,920 | 12,880 |  |
| Allowances |  |  | 20,200 |

# *Basis periods and partnerships*

## Task 3.1

Her first tax year is:

| 2012/13 |
|---|

Her taxable profits in her first year of trading are:

| £ | 6,188 |
|---|---|

Her taxable profits in her second year of trading are:

| £ | 24,750 |
|---|---|

Her taxable profits in her third tax year of trading are:

| £ | 24,750 |
|---|---|

Overlap profits are:

| £ | 22,688 |
|---|---|

(1)   Taxable profits

| Tax year | Basis period | Taxable profits £ |
|---|---|---|
| 2012/13 | (1.1.13– 5.4.13) £33,000 × $^3/_{16}$ = | **6,188** |
| 2013/14 | (6.4.13– 5.4.14) £33,000 × $^{12}/_{16}$ = | **24,750** |
| 2014/15 | (1.5.13 – 30.4.14) £33,000 × $^{12}/_{16}$ = | **24,750** |

(2)   Overlap profits

The profits taxed twice are those for the period 1 May 2013 to 5 April 2014:

$^{11}/_{16}$ × £33,000

## Task 3.2

Mr Phone's basis period for 2012/13 runs from: (insert the date as xx/xx/xxxx)

| 01/07/2012 |

to:

| 05/04/2013 |

Mr Phone's basis period for 2013/14 runs from: (insert the date as xx/xx/xxxx)

| 01/07/2012 |

to:

| 30/06/2013 |

His taxable profits in his second tax year of trading are:

| £ | 23,500 |

Overlap profits are:

| £ | 19,500 |

(1)

| Tax year | Basis period | Taxable profits |
|----------|--------------|-----------------|
| 2012/13: | Actual | £ |
| | 1 July 2012 to 5 April 2013 | |
| | (9/11 × £22,000) | 18,000 |
| 2013/14: | First 12 months | |
| | 1 July 2012 to 30 June 2013 | |
| | £22,000 + (1/12 × £18,000) | 23,500 |
| 2014/15: | (CYB) | |
| | Year ended 31 May 2014 | 18,000 |

(2)

|  | £ |
|--|--|
| Overlap period is 1 July 2012 to 5 April 2013 | 18,000 |
| and 1 June 2013 to 30 June 2013 | |
| (1/12 × £18,000) | 1,500 |
| | 19,500 |

## Task 3.3

Mr Mug's final tax year is: (insert as xxxx/xx)

| 2014/15 |
|---|

Mr Mug's penultimate tax year is: (insert as xxxx/xx)

| 2013/14 |
|---|

His taxable profits in his final tax year of trading are:

| £ | 11,000 |
|---|---|

| Working: | | £ |
|---|---|---|
| 2014/15 | 1 May 2013 to 31 December 2014 (16,000 + 4,000) | 20,000 |
| | Less overlap relief | (9,000) |
| | | **11,000** |

**Note:** Year ended 30 April 2013 was assessed in 2013/14

•••••••••••••••••••••••••••••••••••••••••••••••••••••••••••••••••••••••••••••••••

## Task 3.4

Jackie's first tax year is: (insert as xxxx/xx)

| 2010/11 |
|---|

Her taxable profits in her first tax year of trading are:

| £ | 13,200 |
|---|---|

Jackie's second tax year is: (insert as xxxx/xx)

| 2011/12 |
|---|

Her taxable profits in her second tax year of trading are:

| £ | 14,400 |
|---|---|

Jackie's final tax year is: (insert as xxxx/xx)

| 2014/15 |
|---|

Her taxable profits in her final tax year of trading are:

| £ | 300 |
|---|---|

Over the life of her business Jackie is assessed on total profits of:

£ | 48,240

| Tax year | Basis period | Taxable profits £ |
|---|---|---|
| 2010/11 | First year – 1.5.10 to 5.4.11 | |
| | 11/15 × £18,000 | 13,200 |
| 2011/12 | Second year 12 months to 31.7.11 (1.8.10 – 31.7.11) | |
| | 12/15 × £18,000 | 14,400 |
| 2012/13 | Third year y/e 31.7.12 | 11,700 |
| 2013/14 | y/e 31.7.13 | 8,640 |
| 2014/15 | | |
| | y/e 31.7.14 | 4,800 |
| | p/e 28.2.15 | 5,100 |
| | | 9,900 |
| | Less overlap profits | (9,600) |
| | | 300 |

*Overlap profits*

Overlap period is 1 August 2010 to 5 April 2011, ie 8/15 × £18,000 = £9,600

# Task 3.5

| | Total £ | Fimbo £ | Florrie £ | Pom £ |
|---|---|---|---|---|
| **12 months to 31 December 2013** | | | | |
| Salary | 5,000 | 5,000 | 0 | 0 |
| Share of profits | 5,000 | 3,000 | 2,000 | 0 |
| Total for year | 10,000 | 8,000 | 2,000 | 0 |
| **12 months to 31 December 2014** | | | | |
| Salary | 5,000 | 5,000 | 0 | 0 |
| Share of profits | 15,000 | 9,000 | 6,000 | 0 |
| Total for year | 20,000 | 14,000 | 6,000 | 0 |
| **12 months to 31 December 2015** | | | | |
| Salary | 6,500 | 6,500 | 0 | 0 |
| Share of profits | 18,500 | 6,167 | 6,167 | 6,166 |
| Total for year | 25,000 | 12,667 | 6,167 | 6,166 |

# Task 3.6

(1)

| | Total £ | John £ | Paul £ | George £ |
|---|---|---|---|---|
| **Period ended 31 July 2012** | | | | |
| Division of profits | 24,300 | 9,720 | 7,290 | 7,290 |
| **Year ended 31 July 2013** | | | | |
| Division of profits | 16,200 | 6,480 | 4,860 | 4,860 |
| **Year ended 31 July 20134** | | | | |
| Division of profits | 14,900 | 5,960 | 4,470 | 4,470 |

(2)

| | John | Paul | George |
| --- | --- | --- | --- |
| | £ | £ | £ |
| 2011/12 | 4,166 | 3,124 | 3,124 |
| 2012/13 | 12,420 | 9,315 | 9,315 |
| 2013/14 | 6,480 | 4,860 | 4,860 |
| 2014/15 | 5,960 | 4,470 | 4,470 |

**Working**:

| | John | Paul | George |
| --- | --- | --- | --- |
| | £ | £ | £ |

*2011/12*

1 January 2012 – 5 April 2012

| 3/7 × £(9,720/7,290/7,290) | 4,166 | 3,124 | 3,124 |
| --- | --- | --- | --- |

*2012/13*

(1 January 2012 to 31 December 2012)

| 1 January 2012 to 31 July 2012 | 9,720 | 7,290 | 7,290 |
| --- | --- | --- | --- |

1 August 2012 to 31 December 2012

| 5/12 × £(6,480/4,860/4,860) | 2,700 | 2,025 | 2,025 |
| --- | --- | --- | --- |
| | 12,420 | 9,315 | 9,315 |

*2013/14*

| Year ended 31 July 2013 | 6,480 | 4,860 | 4,860 |
| --- | --- | --- | --- |

*2014/15*

| Year ended 31 July 2014 | 5,960 | 4,470 | 4,470 |
| --- | --- | --- | --- |

..................................................................................................

## Task 3.7

| Year ended 31 December 2014 | Total £ | Strange £ | Pavin £ | Lehman £ |
|---|---|---|---|---|
| **To 31 July 2014** | | | | |
| Salaries (15,000/5000 × 7/12) | 11,667 | 8,750 | 2,917 | 0 |
| Interest on capital (20,000/10,000 × 5% × 7/12) | 875 | 583 | 292 | 0 |
| Division of profits (48,000 × 7/12 – 11,667 – 875) | 15,458 | 7,729 | 5,153 | 2,576 |
| **To 31 December 2014** | | | | |
| Salary (20,000 × 5/12) | 8,333 | 8,333 | 0 | 0 |
| Division of profits (48,000 × 5/12 – 8,333) | 11,667 | 4,667 | 4,667 | 2,333 |
| Total for year ended 31 December 2014 | 48,000 | 30,062 | 13,029 | 4,909 |

## Task 3.8

| Year ended 31 May 2014 | Total £ | Bob £ | Annie £ | John £ |
|---|---|---|---|---|
| **To 31 January 2014** | | | | |
| Salaries | 30,000 | 10,000 | 10,000 | 10,000 |
| Division of profits | 30,000 | 15,000 | 7,500 | 7,500 |
| **To 31 May 2014** | | | | |
| Salaries | 10,000 | 0 | 5,000 | 5,000 |
| Division of profits | 20,000 | 0 | 10,000 | 10,000 |
| Total for year ended 31 May 2014 | 90,000 | 25,000 | 32,500 | 32,500 |

# Task 3.9

**Working:**

Tax adjusted trading profit for the partnership is:

|  | £ |
|---|---|
| Revenue | 125,000 |
| Cost of goods | (75,000) |
| Rental | (12,000) |
| Admin | (1,700) |
| Accountancy | (650) |
| Goods for own use | 1,550 |
| AIA on sewing machine | (1,200) |
|  | 36,000 |

| Page 6 | |
|---|---|
| Box 1 | 01.01.14 |
| Box 2 | 31.12.14 |
| Box 3 | Retail – designer dresses |
| Box 11 | 36000.00 |
| Box 22 | 8000 |
| Box 25 | 1600 |
| Box 6 | Anne Curtis |
| Box 11 | 18000.00 |
| Box 22 | 4000 |
| Box 25 | 800 |

## Incorporated businesses

### Task 4.1

| | Year to 31 December 2014 | Five months to 31 May 2015 |
|---|---|---|
| | £ | £ |
| Trading profits (12:5) | 352,941 | 147,059 |
| Property business income (12:5) | 10,800 | 4,500 |
| Chargeable gain | 0 | 3,000 |
| Total profits | 363,741 | 154,559 |
| Qualifying charitable donations paid | (30,000) | (40,000) |
| Taxable total profits | 333,741 | 114,559 |

#### Tutor's notes

(1) Trading profits are time apportioned.
(2) Property business income is time apportioned.
(3) Chargeable gains are allocated to the period in which they are realised.
(4) Qualifying charitable donations are allocated to the period in which they are paid.

### Task 4.2

| | Time apportioned | Period in which arises | Separate computation |
|---|---|---|---|
| Capital allowances | | | ✓ |
| Trading income | ✓ | | |
| Property income | ✓ | | |
| Interest income | | ✓ | |
| Chargeable gain | | ✓ | |

# Task 4.3

(1) The upper limit for marginal relief for T Ltd will be:

| £ | 200,000 |
|---|---------|

(£1,500,000/5 × 8/12)

(2) The lower limit for marginal relief for T Ltd will be:

| £ | 40,000 |
|---|--------|

(£300,000/5 × 8/12)

(3) The corporation tax payable is:

| £ | 7,623 |
|---|-------|

Marginal relief applies (FY14).

| | £ |
|---|---|
| £38,000 × 21% | 7,980 |
| Less 1/400 £(200,000 – 42,000) × £38,000/ £42,000 | (357) |
| Corporation tax payable | 7,623 |

# Task 4.4

(1) The augmented profits for Rosemary Ltd are:

| £ | 1,080,000 |
|---|-----------|

| | £ |
|---|---|
| Trading profits | 600,000 |
| Property business income | 300,000 |
| Taxable total profits | 900,000 |
| Dividends received × 100/90 | 180,000 |
| Augmented profits | 1,080,000 |

(2) The upper limit for marginal relief for Rosemary Ltd will be:

| £ | 1,250,000 |
|---|---|

£1,500,000 × 10/12

(3) The lower limit for marginal relief for Rosemary Ltd will be:

| £ | 250,000 |
|---|---|

£300,000 × 10/12

(4)

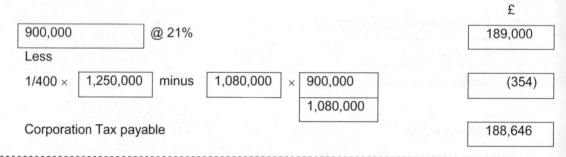

|  |  | £ |
|---|---|---|
| 900,000 @ 21% | | 189,000 |
| Less | | |
| 1/400 × 1,250,000 minus 1,080,000 × 900,000 / 1,080,000 | | (354) |
| Corporation Tax payable | | 188,646 |

## Task 4.5

(1) The taxable total profits for Island Ltd are:

| £ | 360,000 |
|---|---|

(2) The upper limit for marginal relief for Island Ltd will be:

| £ | 333,333 |
|---|---|

(3) The corporation tax payable is:

| £ | 75,600 |
|---|---|

|  | £ |
|---|---|
| Trading profits | 300,000 |
| Chargeable gain | 60,000 |
| Taxable total profits/augmented profits | 360,000 |

Upper limit $\dfrac{1,500,000}{3} \times 8/12 = £333,333$

As augmented profits are above the upper limit the main rate of tax (for FY14) applies:

£360,000 × 21% = **£75,600**

......................................................................................................

## Task 4.6

(1) The augmented profits for Basil Ltd are:

| £ | 1,130,000 |
|---|---|

|  | *9 months to 30 June 2014* |
|---|---|
|  | £ |
| Trading profits | 1,000,000 |
| Chargeable gains | 120,000 |
| Taxable total profits | 1,120,000 |
| Dividends received × 100/90 | 10,000 |
| Augmented profits | 1,130,000 |

(2) The upper limit for marginal relief for Basil Ltd will be:

| £ | 1,125,000 |
|---|---|

(1,500,000 × 9/12)

(3) The corporation tax payable is:

| £ | 250,133 |
|---|---|

**FY13 :** £1,120,000 × 6/9 × 23% = 171,733

**FY14 :** £1,120,000 × 3/9 × 21% = 78,400

**Total corporation tax payable: = £250,133**

......................................................................................................

## Task 4.7

Total turnover (box 1): £525000.00

Taxable trading profits (box 3): £394000.00

Net trading profits (box 5): £394000.00

Interest (box 6): £3000.00

Property business income (box 11): £16000.00

Profits (box 21): £413000.00

Taxable total profits (box 37): £413000.00

Marginal relief (box 42): X

Financial year (box 43): 2014

Amount of profit (box 44): £413000.00

Rate of tax (box 45): 21.00

Tax (box 46): £86,730.00

Corporation tax (box 63): £86,730.00

Marginal rate relief (box 64): £2,717.50

Corporation tax net of marginal rate relief (box 65): £84,012.50

Corporation tax chargeable (box 70): £84,012.50

# Losses

## Task 5.1

|  | 2012/13 | 2013/14 | 2014/15 | 2015/16 |
|---|---|---|---|---|
|  | £ | £ | £ | £ |
| Trading profits | 12,000 | 0 | 8,000 | 14,000 |
| Trading loss offset against future year | 0 | 0 | (8,000) | (3,600) |
| Property income | 10,400 | 11,000 | 11,000 | 11,000 |
| Trading loss offset against current year | 0 . | (11,000) | 0 | 0 |
| Trading loss offset against previous year | (22,400) | 0 | 0 | 0 |
| Net income | 0 | 0 | 11,000 | 21,400 |

## Task 5.2

|  | ✓ |
|---|---|
| True |  |
| False | ✓ |

An individual cannot restrict a claim to set a trading loss against total income in order to have enough net income to use his personal allowance – the loss must be set-off as far as possible even if this means that the personal allowance is not available.

## Task 5.3

|  | ✓ |
|---|---|
| True |  |
| False | ✓ |

An individual does not have to make a trading loss claim against total income in the tax year of the loss before making a claim to set the loss against total income in the preceding year – a claim can be made for either year or both years.

## Task 5.4

|  | ✓ |
|-------|---|
| True | ✓ |
| False |  |

An individual can only carry a trading loss forward against trading income of the same trade.

............................................................................

## Task 5.5

|  | Year ended 30 June | | |
|--|--|--|--|
|  | 2012 | 2013 | 2014 |
| Trading profits | 62,000 | 20,000 | 0 |
| Interest | 1,200 | 600 | 1,200 |
| Total profits | 63,200 | 20,600 | 1,200 |
| Current period loss relief | 0 | 0 | (1,200) |
| Carry back loss relief | 0 | (20,600) | 0 |
| Total profits after loss relief | 63,200 | 0 | 0 |
| Qualifying charitable donation | (100) | 0 | 0 |
| Taxable total profits | 63,100 | 0 | 0 |

(2)  The trading loss available to carry forward at 30 June 2014 is:

| £ | 61,200 |
|---|--------|

(£83,000 – £1,200 – £20,600)

............................................................................

# Task 5.6

|  | Year ended 30.9.12 | 9 months to 30.6.13 | Year ended 30.6.14 | Year ended 30.6.15 |
|---|---|---|---|---|
| Trading profits | 6,200 | 4,320 | 0 | 53,000 |
| Carry forward loss relief | 0 | 0 | 0 | (53,000) |
| Interest | 80 | 240 | 260 | 200 |
| Property income | 1,420 | 1,440 | 1,600 | 1,500 |
| Chargeable gains | 0 | 7,680 | 0 | 0 |
| Total profits | 7,700 | 13,680 | 1,860 | 1,700 |
| Current period loss relief | 0 | 0 | (1,860) | 0 |
| Carry back loss relief | (1,925) | (13,680) | 0 | 0 |
| Total profits after loss relief | 5,775 | 0 | 0 | 1,700 |
| Qualifying charitable donation | (1,000) | 0 | 0 | (1,500) |
| Taxable total profits | 4,775 | 0 | 0 | 200 |

**Tutor's note**. The loss can be carried back to set against profits arising in the previous 12 months. This means that the set-off in the y/e 30.9.12 is restricted to 3/12 × £7,700 = £1,925.

(2) The trading loss available to carry forward at 30 June 2015 is:

| £ | 29,535 |
|---|---|

(£100,000 – £1,860 – £13,680 – £1,925 – £53,000)

(3) The capital loss available to carry forward at 30 June 2015 is:

| £ | 9,423 |
|---|---|

# Task 5.7

|  | ✓ |
|---|---|
| True | ✓ |
| False |  |

A company must offset its trading loss against total profits in the loss-making period before carrying the loss back.

## Task 5.8

| | ✓ |
|---|---|
| True | |
| False | ✓ |

If a company carries a trading loss forward, the loss can only be set against trading profits from the same trade.

••••••••••••••••••••••••••••••••••••••••••••••••••••••••••••••••••••••••••••••••••••

## Task 5.9

| | ✓ |
|---|---|
| True | |
| False | ✓ |

A company can set-off a capital loss against capital gains only.

••••••••••••••••••••••••••••••••••••••••••••••••••••••••••••••••••••••••••••••••••••

# National insurance

## Task 6.1

The Class 2 NIC liability for 2014/15 is:

| £ | 143 | • | 00 |
|---|-----|---|----|

The Class 4 NIC liability for 2014/15 is:

| £ | 438 | • | 66 |
|---|-----|---|----|

The total NIC liability for 2014/15 is:

| £ | 581 | • | 66 |
|---|-----|---|----|

|  | £ |
|---|---|
| Profits | 12,830 |
| Less lower profits limit | (7,956) |
| Excess | 4,874 |

Class 4 NICs (9% × £4,874)     = £438.66

Class 2 NICs = £2.75 × 52     = £143.00

Total NICs £(438.66 + 143.00)     = **£581.66**

····················································································

## Task 6.2

The Class 2 NIC liability for 2014/15 is:

| £ | 143 | • | 00 |
|---|-----|---|----|

The Class 4 NIC liability for 2014/15 is:

| £ | 3,174 | • | 51 |
|---|-------|---|----|

The total NIC liability for 2014/15 is:

| £ | 3,317 | • | 51 |
|---|-------|---|----|

|  | £ |
|---|---|
| Upper profits limit | 41,865 |
| Less: lower profits limit | (7,956) |
| Excess | 33,909 |

|  | £ |
|---|---|
| Class 4 NICs (9% × £33,909) | 3,051.81 |
| + 2% × £(48,000 − 41,865) | 122.70 |
|  | 3,174.51 |

Class 2 NICs = £2.75 × 52      = <u>£143.00</u>

Total NICs £(3,174.51 + 143.00)      = **£3,317.51**

## Task 6.3

The Class 2 NIC liability for 2014/15 is:

| £ | 0 | • | 0 |
|---|---|---|---|

The Class 4 NIC liability for 2014/15 is:

| £ | 0 | • | 0 |
|---|---|---|---|

The total NIC liability for 2014/15 is:

| £ | 0 | • | 0 |
|---|---|---|---|

As Raj's trading profits are below the lower profits limit, there is no liability to Class 4 NICs. He is also excepted from payment of Class 2 NICs because his **accounting profits** are below the small earnings exception limit.

## Task 6.4

(1) The date by which Zoe must notify that she is liable to Class 2 NICs is: (insert the date as xx/xx/xxxx)

31/01/2016

A self-employed person must notify HMRC that she is liable to Class 2 NICs by 31 January following the end of the tax year in which he or she becomes self-employed.

(2)

The Class 2 NIC liability for 2014/15 is:

| £ | 143 | • | 00 |

The Class 4 NIC liability for 2014/15 is:

| £ | 3,814 | • | 51 |

The total NIC liability for 2014/15 is:

| £ | 3,957 | • | 51 |

Class 2 = £2.75 × 52 = <u>£143.00</u>

|  |  | £ |
|---|---|---|
| Class4 | £(41,865 – 7,956) × 9% (main) | 3,051.81 |
|  | £(80,000 – 41,865) × 2% (additional) | <u>762.70</u> |
|  |  | <u>3,814.51</u> |

Total NICs £(<u>3,814.51</u> + <u>143.00</u>) = **£3,957.51**

## Task 6.5

(1)  The share of profits taxable on Paula for 2014/15 is:

| £ | 8,000 |

Share of profits for y/e 31.12.15 is £160,000 × 20% = £32,000
Basis period for 2014/15 = 1.1.15 to 5.4.15 (3/12 × £32,000 = £8,000)

and for 2015/16 is:

| £ | 32,000 |

Basis period for 2015/16 = 1.1.15 to 31.12.15

and the overlap profits to carry forward are:

| £ | 8,000 |

1.1.15 to 5.4.15 (3/12 × £32,000 = £8,000)

(2)  The Class 4 National Insurance Contributions payable by Paula for 2014/15 are:

| £ | 3 | • | 96 |

£(8,000 – 7,956) = £44 × 9%

# Tax administration

## Task 7.1

| | ✓ |
|---|---|
| 31 January 2016 | ✓ |
| 5 April 2016 | |
| 31 October 2015 | |
| 31 December 2015 | |

## Task 7.2

| | ✓ |
|---|---|
| The full amount of £20,500 will be paid on 31 January 2016. | |
| Payments on account based on the estimated 2014/15 liability will be made on 31 January and 31 July 2015, with the balance payable on 31 January 2016. | |
| Payments on account of £10,250 will be made on 31 January and 31 July 2015 with nothing due on 31 January 2016. | |
| Payments on account of £7,250 will be made on 31 January and 31 July 2015, with the balance of £6,000 being paid on 31 January 2016. | ✓ |

## Task 7.3

| | ✓ |
|---|---|
| 100% | |
| 50% | ✓ |
| 35% | |
| 15% | |

## Task 7.4

| | ✓ |
|---|---|
| 0% | |
| 20% | |
| 30% | ✓ |
| 35% | |

## Task 7.5

| | ✓ |
|---|---|
| True | ✓ |
| False | |

The return is filed less than 3 months after the due filing date.

## Task 7.6

| | ✓ |
|---|---|
| True | ✓ |
| False | |

The penalty for failure to keep records is £3,000 per tax year or accounting period.

## Task 7.7

| | ✓ |
|---|---|
| True | |
| False | ✓ |

Penalties for late payment do not apply to payments on account.

## Task 7.8

| Instalment | Due date | Amount due (£) |
| --- | --- | --- |
| 1 | 14/10/2014 | 125,000 |
| 2 | 14/01/2015 | 125,000 |
| 3 | 14/04/2015 | 125,000 |
| 4 | 14/07/2015 | 125,000 |

## Task 7.9

| | True | False |
| --- | --- | --- |
| A company with a period of account ending on 31 March 2015 must keep its records until 31 March 2017. | | ✓ (until 31 March 2021) |
| The due date for payment of CGT for 2014/15 is 31 January 2016. | ✓ | |
| An individual who becomes chargeable to income tax in 2014/15 must notify HMRC by 31 October 2015. | | ✓ (by 5 October 2015) |
| A large company will not have to pay corporation tax by instalments if it has augmented profits not exceeding £10m and was not large in the previous accounting period. | ✓ | |
| A company which pays corporation tax at the small profits rate must pay its corporation tax by nine months and one day after the end of its accounting period. | ✓ | |

# Chargeable gains – the basics

## Task 8.1

For the gain on the disposal of a capital asset to be a chargeable gain there must be a chargeable | disposal | of a chargeable | asset | by a chargeable | person |.

## Task 8.2

| Item | Chargeable | Exempt |
|---|---|---|
| Wasting chattel with useful life of 25 years | | ✓ |
| Disposal of half the holding of a plot of land | ✓ | |
| Car used for business purposes | | ✓ |

## Task 8.3

| | ✓ |
|---|---|
| £34,000 | ✓ |
| £39,000 | |
| £45,000 | |
| £50,000 | |

| | £ |
|---|---|
| Proceeds of sale | 90,000 |
| Less cost | (40,000) |
| Less enhancement expenditure | (5,000) |
| Chargeable gain | 45,000 |
| Less annual exempt amount | (11,000) |
| Taxable gain | 34,000 |

# Task 8.4

(1) George's capital gains tax liability for 2014/15 is:

| £ | 1,523 |
|---|---|

| | £ |
|---|---|
| Chargeable gains | 20,000 |
| Less allowable losses | (3,560) |
| Net chargeable gains | 16,440 |
| Less annual exempt amount | (11,000) |
| Taxable gains | 5,440 |
| CGT @ 28% | **£1,523** |

(2) George's capital gains tax liability is payable by:

| 31 January 2016 |
|---|

# Task 8.5

The amount of the loss Graham will use in 2014/15 is:

| £ | 5,200 |
|---|---|

**Note:** Current year losses cannot be restricted in order to get the benefit of the annual exempt amount.

| | £ |
|---|---|
| Chargeable gains | 15,000 |
| Less allowable losses | (5,200) |
| Net chargeable gains | 9,800 |
| Less annual exempt amount | (11,000) |
| Taxable gains | 0 |

## Task 8.6

Gayle's capital gains tax liability for 2014/15 is:

| £ | 2,160 |
|---|-------|

|                              | £        |
|------------------------------|----------|
|                              | £        |
| Chargeable gains             | 22,500   |
| Less allowable losses        | (2,000)  |
| Net chargeable gains         | 20,500   |
| Less annual exempt amount    | (11,000) |
| Taxable gains                | 9,500    |
| CGT payable                  |          |

|                  | £     |
|------------------|-------|
| £5,000 @ 18%     | 900   |
| £4,500 @ 28%     | 1,260 |
|                  | **2,160** |

## Task 8.7

Gerry's capital gains tax liability for 2014/15 is:

| £ | 3,585 |
|---|-------|

|                              | £        |
|------------------------------|----------|
| Chargeable gains             | 27,000   |
| Less annual exempt amount    | (11,000) |
| Taxable gains                | 16,000   |

| CGT              | £     |
|------------------|-------|
| £8,955 (W) @ 18% | 1,612 |
| £7,045 @ 28%     | 1,973 |
|                  | **3,585** |

(W) Unused basic rate band is £31,865 − £22,910 = £8,955

## Task 8.8

The losses to carry forward to 2015/16 are:

| £ | 4,800 |
|---|-------|

(5,000 – 200)

|  | £ |
|--|--:|
| Gains | 17,800 |
| Losses | (6,600) |
|  | 11,200 |
| Losses b/f (11,200 – 11,000) | (200) |
|  | 11,000 |
| Less annual exempt amount | (11,000) |
| Taxable gains | NIL |

---

## Task 8.9

The maximum allowable loss carried forward to 2015/16 will be:

| £ | 11,300 |
|---|--------|

| Tax year | 2012/13 | 2013/14 | 2014/15 |
|----------|---------|---------|---------|
|  | £ | £ | £ |
| Gains | 2,000 | 4,000 | 13,700 |
| Losses | (14,000) | (2,000) | (2,000) |
| Net gain/(loss) | (12,000) | 2,000 | 11,700 |
| Less loss b/f | (0) | 0 | (700) |
| Less annual exempt amount | 0 | (2,000) | (11,000) |
| Chargeable gain | 0 | 0 | 0 |
|  |  |  |  |
| Loss c/f | (12,000) | (12,000) | (11,300) |

The use of the loss brought forward in 2014/15 is restricted to the amount of the annual exempt amount.

---

## Task 8.10

|  | £ |
|---|---|
| Proceeds | 230,000 |
| Less cost | (140,000) |
| Unindexed gain | 90,000 |
| Less indexation allowance 0.819 × £140,000 (restricted) | (90,000) |
| Chargeable gain/allowable loss | 0 |

## Task 8.11

|  | £ |
|---|---|
| Proceeds | 180,000 |
| Less   cost | (100,000) |
|      enhancement expenditure | (25,000) |
| Unindexed gain | 55,000 |
| Less   indexation allowance on cost 0.375 × £100,000 | (37,500) |
|      indexation allowance on enhancement  0.287 × £25,000 | (7,175) |
| Chargeable gain | 10,325 |

## Task 8.12

|  | ✓ |
|---|---|
| True |  |
| False | ✓ |

Individuals are entitled to an annual exempt amount but not companies.

# Further aspects of chargeable gains

## Task 9.1

(1) The cost of the land sold is:

| £ | 120,000 |
|---|---------|

$$\frac{240,000}{240,000 + 60,000} \times £150,000$$

(2) The gain on sale is:

| £ | 117,000 |
|---|---------|

|  | £ |
|---|---:|
| Disposal proceeds | 240,000 |
| Less   disposal costs | (3,000) |
| Net proceeds | 237,000 |
| Less   cost | (120,000) |
| Chargeable gain | **117,000** |

...................................................................................................................

## Task 9.2

Her chargeable gain on sale is:

|  | ✓ |
|---|---|
| £2,300 |  |
| £2,000 |  |
| £2,500 |  |
| £1,700 | ✓ |

|  | £ |
|---|---:|
| Gross proceeds | 7,500 |
| Less   costs of sale | (300) |
| Net proceeds | 7,200 |
| Less   cost | (5,500) |
| Chargeable gain | 1,700 |
| Gain cannot exceed 5/3 × £(7,500 – 6,000) | 2,500 |

...................................................................................................................

## Task 9.3

Mark's allowable loss is:

| £ | 3,500 |
|---|-------|

| | £ |
|---|---|
| Deemed proceeds | 6,000 |
| Less   costs of sale £(4,500 × 100/90) = £5,000 × 10% | (500) |
| Net proceeds | 5,500 |
| Less   cost | (9,000) |
| Allowable loss | **(3,500)** |

## Task 9.4

| | ✓ |
|---|---|
| True | |
| False | ✓ |

The proceeds are less than £6,000 so the gain is exempt.

## Task 9.5

John's chargeable gains (before the annual exempt amount) for 2014/15 are:

| | ✓ |
|---|---|
| £45,000 | ✓ |
| £30,000 | |
| £34,100 | |
| £19,100 | |

The gain on the disposal to John's brother is £(60,000 – 15,000) = £45,000. The loss on the disposal to John's daughter can only be set against disposals to that connected person.

## Task 9.6

|  | ✓ |
|---|---|
| True | ✓ |
| False |  |

Disposals to connected persons are at market value.

························································································

## Task 9.7

(1)   The cost of the two offices disposed of is:

| £ | 76,087 |
|---|---|

$$£250,000 \times \frac{140,000}{140,000 + 320,000}$$

(2)   The chargeable gain arising on the disposal is:

| £ | 26,783 |
|---|---|

|  | £ |
|---|---|
| Proceeds | 140,000 |
| Less   cost | (76,087) |
|  | 63,913 |
|  |  |
| Less   IA |  |
| 0.488 × £76,087 | (37,130) |
| Chargeable gain | **26,783** |

························································································

## Task 9.8

| | £ |
|---|---|
| Proceeds | 8,000 |
| Disposal costs | (500) |
| Cost of acquisition | (4,500) |
| Indexation allowance (4,500 × 0.291) | (1,310) |
| Gain | 1,690 |
| Gain using chattel marginal relief 5/3 (8,000 – 6,000) | 3,333 |
| Chargeable gain (lower of actual gain and marginal relief) | 1,690 |

## Shares

### Task 10.1

His net gain on sale is:

| £ | 9,800 |
|---|---|

Match acquisition in next 30 days first

|  | £ |
|---|---|
| Proceeds of sale £20,000 × 1,000/5,000 | 4,000 |
| Less   cost | (4,200) |
| Loss | (200) |

Then match with share pool

|  | £ |
|---|---|
| Proceeds of sale £20,000 × 4,000/5,000 | 16,000 |
| Less   cost £9,000 × 4,000/6,000 | (6,000) |
| Gain | 10,000 |

........................................................................................

### Task 10.2

*Share pool*

|  | No of shares | Cost |
|---|---|---|
|  |  | £ |
| 10 February 1999 | 12,000 | 18,000 |
| 20 September 2006 Bonus 1:4 | 3,000 | 0 |
| Total before disposal | 15,000 | 18,000 |
| 15 March 2015 Disposal | (2,000) | (2,400) |
| c/f | 13,000 | 15,600 |

*Gain on sale*

|  | £ |
|---|---|
| Proceeds | 8,000 |
| Less: cost | (2,400) |
| Gain | 5,600 |

## Task 10.3

*Share pool*

|  | No of shares | Cost |
|---|---|---|
|  |  | £ |
| 9 December 1999: purchase | 12,000 | 4,400 |
| 12 October 2003 Rights 1:3@ £5 | 4,000 | 20,000 |
| Total before disposal | 16,000 | 24,400 |
| 4 November 2014 Disposal | (8,000) | (12,200) |
| c/f | 8,000 | 12,200 |

*Gains on sale*

|  | £ | £ |
|---|---|---|
| *Next 30 days* |  |  |
| Proceeds (2,000/10,000 × 60,000) | 12,000 |  |
| Cost | (11,500) |  |
| Gain/(loss) |  | 500 |
| *Share pool* |  |  |
| Proceeds (8,000/10,000 × 60,000) | 48,000 |  |
| Cost | (12,200) |  |
| Gain/(loss) |  | 35,800 |
| Total gain/(loss) |  | 36,300 |

## Task 10.4

*FA 1985 pool*

|  | No of shares | Original cost | Indexed cost |
|---|---|---|---|
| *September 1993* |  | £ | £ |
| Acquisition | 5,000 | 10,000 | 10,000 |
| *October 2003* |  |  |  |
| Indexed rise 0.287 × £10,000 |  |  | 2,870 |
| Rights 1:5 @ £5 | 1,000 | 5,000 | 5,000 |
|  | 6,000 | 15,000 | 17,870 |
| *August 2004* |  |  |  |
| Indexed rise 0.026 × £17,870 |  |  | 465 |
| Acquisition | 14,000 | 84,000 | 84,000 |
|  | 20,000 | 99,000 | 102,335 |
| *January 2015* |  |  |  |
| Indexed rise 0.384 × £102,335 |  |  | 39,297 |
|  |  |  | 141,632 |
| Sale (99,000/141,632 × 18000/20,000) | (18,000) | (89,100) | (127,469) |
| c/f | 2,000 | 9,900 | 14,163 |

*Gain*

|  | £ |
|---|---|
| Proceeds | 155,000 |
| Less   cost | (89,100) |
|  | 65,900 |
| Less   indexation allowance £(127,469 – 89,100) | (38,369) |
| Chargeable gain | 27,531 |

# Task 10.5

*FA 1985 pool*

|  | No of shares | Cost | Indexed cost |
|---|---|---|---|
|  |  | £ | £ |
| *26 May 1995* |  |  |  |
| Acquisition | 4,000 | 24,000 | 24,000 |
| *30 June 1996* Bonus issue (1/2 × 4,000) | 2,000 |  |  |
| *24 October 2003* |  |  |  |
| Indexed rise  0.221 × £24,000 |  |  | 5,304 |
| Acquisition | 5,000 | 27,500 | 27,500 |
| c/f | 11,000 | 51,500 | 56,804 |
| *25 May 2014* |  |  |  |
| Indexed rise  0.401 × £56,804 |  |  | 22,778 |
|  |  |  | 79,582 |
| Disposal | (11,000) | (51,500) | (79,582) |
| c/f | 0 | 0 | 0 |

*Gain*

|  | £ |
|---|---|
| Proceeds | 78,200 |
| Less cost | (51,500) |
|  | 26,700 |
| Less indexation allowance £(79,582 − 51,500) | (28,082) |
| Gain | nil |

## Task 10.6

| | ✓ |
|---|---|
| True | ✓ |
| False | |

Indexation allowance on rights issue shares runs from the date of the rights issue even though the rights issue shares are treated as having been acquired at the time of the original acquisition to which they relate.

# Reliefs for gains

## Task 11.1

| | £ | £ |
|---|---|---|
| Proceeds of goodwill | 50,000 | |
| Less cost | 0 | |
| Gain/(loss) on goodwill | | 50,000 |
| | | |
| Proceeds of shop | 90,000 | |
| Less cost | (80,000) | |
| Gain/(loss) on shop | | 10,000 |
| Proceeds of warehouse | 130,000 | |
| Less cost | (150,000) | |
| Gain/(loss) on warehouse | | (20,000) |
| Net gains eligible for entrepreneurs' relief | | 40,000 |
| Less annual exempt amount | | (11,000) |
| Taxable gains | | 29,000 |
| CGT payable @ 10% | | 2,900 |

## Task 11.2

| | ✓ |
|---|---|
| True | ✓ |
| False | |

The lifetime limit of gains eligible for entrepreneurs' relief is £10,000,000.

# Task 11.3

The taxable gain arising on the sale of the Blue Ltd shares is:

| £ | 139,000 |
|---|---------|

|                            | £        | £        |
|----------------------------|----------|----------|
|                            |          |          |
| Proceeds                   |          | 200,000  |
| Less cost                  | 65,000   |          |
| Less gain rolled over      | (15,000) |          |
|                            |          | (50,000) |
| Chargeable gain            |          | 150,000  |
| Less annual exempt amount  |          | (11,000) |
| Taxable gain               |          | **139,000** |

# Task 11.4

(1)  Fran's chargeable gain on her disposal is:

| £ | 0 |
|---|---|

|                            | £         |
|----------------------------|-----------|
| Proceeds (MV) June 2014    | 500,000   |
| Less cost                  | (75,000)  |
| Gain                       | 425,000   |
| Less gift relief           | (425,000) |
| Gain left in charge        | **0**     |

(2) Anna's chargeable gain on her disposal is:

£ | 445,000

| | £ | £ |
|---|---|---|
| Proceeds July 2015 | | 520,000 |
| Cost (MV) | 500,000 | |
| Less gift relief gain (from above) | (425,000) | |
| Base cost | | (75,000) |
| Chargeable gain | | **445,000** |

## Task 11.5

(1) Edward's gain on the disposal before rollover relief is:

£ | 65,000

| | £ |
|---|---|
| Proceeds | 125,000 |
| Less cost | (60,000) |
| Gain | **65,000** |

(2) Assuming rollover relief is claimed, the gain immediately chargeable is:

£ | 1,500

Proceeds not re-invested (£125,000 – £123,500)

(3) The gain which Edward can rollover into the new premises is:

£ | £63,500

| | £ |
|---|---|
| Gain | 65,000 |
| Less immediately chargeable | (1,500) |
| Gain rolled-over against new premises | 63,500 |

## Task 11.6

(1) The gain on disposal in May 2011 was:

| £ | 73,050 |
|---|--------|

| | £ |
|---|---|
| Proceeds | 145,000 |
| Less cost | (50,000) |
| | 95,000 |
| Less indexation allowance 0.439 × £50,000 | (21,950) |
| Chargeable gain | **73,050** |

(2) The gain available for rollover relief is:

| £ | 68,050 |
|---|--------|

| | £ |
|---|---|
| Gain | 73,050 |
| Less chargeable in 2011 | |
| Proceeds not reinvested = £(145,000 – 140,000) | (5,000) |
| Gain available for rollover relief | **68,050** |

(3) The base cost of the property acquired in April 2014 is:

| £ | 71,950 |
|---|--------|

| | £ |
|---|---|
| Cost of new property | 140,000 |
| Less gain rolled over | (68,050) |
| Base cost of new property | **71,950** |

## Task 11.7

If L plc wishes to claim rollover relief it must acquire a new asset between:

| | ✓ |
|---|---|
| The start of the previous accounting period and the end of the next accounting period | |
| Three years before and three years after the date of the disposal | |
| One year before and three years after the date of the disposal | ✓ |
| One year before and one year after the date of the disposal | |

BPP
LEARNING MEDIA

# AAT AQ2013
# SAMPLE ASSESSMENT
# BUSINESS TAX

**Time allowed: 2 hours**

# Business Tax AAT (AQ2013) sample assessment

We have provided the following sample assessment to help you familiarise yourself with AAT's e-assessment environment. It is designed to demonstrate as many as possible of the question types you may find in a live assessment. It is not designed to be used on its own to determine whether you are ready for a live assessment.

This assessment comprises 11 tasks.

You should attempt and aim to complete EVERY task in EACH section.

Each task is independent. You will not need to refer to your answers to previous tasks.

Read every task carefully to make sure you understand what is required.

Please note that in this assessment only your responses to task 1, 3, 4, 5, 6 and 9 will be marked.

Equivalents of tasks 2, 7, 8 and 10 will be human marked in the live assessment.

Where the date is relevant, it is given in the task data.

Both minus signs and brackets can be used to indicate negative numbers UNLESS task instructions say otherwise.

You must use a full stop to indicate a decimal point.

For example, write 100.57 NOT 100,57 or 100 57

You may use a comma to indicate a number in the thousands, but you don't have to.

For example, 10000 and 10,000 are both OK.

Other indicators are not compatible with the computer-marked system.

There are two tables of tax data provided in this assessment. You can access these at any point by clicking on the buttons found in every task. The buttons will appear at the top of each task, and look like this:

When you click on a button, the table will appear in a pop-up window. You can then move or close the window.

When you move on to a new task, you will have to re-open a window to see the data again.

The taxation data is also available in this introduction, and can be accessed at any time during the assessment by clicking on the introduction button on the bottom left of the assessment window.

# Business Tax AAT (AQ2013) sample assessment

## TAXATION DATA

**Taxation tables for Business Tax – 2014/15**

**Note that 'TAXATION DATA 1' and 'TAXATION DATA 2' shown below will be available as pop up windows throughout your live assessment.**

### TAXATION DATA 1

*Capital allowances*
Annual investment allowance

| | |
|---|---:|
| From 1 January 2013 | £250,000 |
| From 1/6 April 2014 | £500,000 |
| Plant and machinery writing down allowance | 18% |

Motor cars

| | |
|---|---:|
| $CO_2$ emissions up to 95g/km | 100% |
| $CO_2$ emissions between 96g/km and 130g/km | 18% |
| $CO_2$ emissions over 130g/km | 8% |

Energy efficient and water saving plant

| | |
|---|---:|
| First year allowance | 100% |

*Capital gains*

| | |
|---|---:|
| Annual exempt amount | £11,000 |
| Standard rate | 18% |
| Higher rate (applicable over £31,865) | 28% |
| Entrepreneurs' relief rate | 10% |
| Entrepreneurs' relief limit | £10,000,000 |

*National insurance rates*

| | |
|---|---:|
| Class 2 contributions: | £2.75 per week |
| Small earnings exception | £5,885 p.a. |
| Class 4 contributions: | |
| Main rate | 9% |
| Additional rate | 2% |
| Lower profits limit | £7,956 |
| Upper profits limit | £41,865 |

### TAXATION DATA 2

*Corporate tax*

| *Corporation tax* | | |
|---|---|---|
| Financial year | *2014* | *2013* |
| Small profits rate | 20% | 20% |
| Marginal relief: | | |
| Lower limit | £300,000 | £300,000 |
| Upper limit | £1,500,000 | £1,500,000 |
| Standard fraction | 1/400 | 3/400 |
| Main rate | 21% | 23% |

Marginal relief formula: Fraction × (U–A) ×
N/A

## Task 1 (12 marks)

Lynsey has the following income statement:

| | £ | £ |
|---|---|---|
| Gross profit | | 1,540,745 |
| Wages and salaries | 856,850 | |
| Accountancy and legal costs (Note 1) | 23,160 | |
| Motor expenses | 75,560 | |
| Repairs and renewals (Note 2) | 59,230 | |
| Office expenses | 39,920 | |
| Depreciation | 148,860 | |
| Other expenses (Note 3) | 32,840 | 1,236,420 |
| Profit | | 304,325 |

Notes include:

| 1 | Accountancy and legal costs include: | £ |
|---|---|---|
| | Annual accounting and audit fee. | 13,000 |
| | Legal costs in connection with a successful tax appeal. | 8,690 |
| 2 | Repairs and renewals include: | |
| | Redecoration of the administrative offices. | 10,500 |
| | Cost of installing a new machine. | 14,130 |
| 3 | Other expenses include: | |
| | Donation to a local charity that uses mugs with Lynsey's business logo. | 1,000 |
| | Cost of Easter eggs given to customers free if they order more than 10 items. | 800 |
| | Cost of bottles of wine given to customers if their order is over £3,000. The business logo is on the back of the bottle. | 1,400 |
| | Customer entertainment. | 2,450 |
| 4 | Capital allowances have already been calculated at: | 142,950 |

(a) **Complete the computation. Do not use minus signs or brackets to show negative figures. Please keep your selected answers in the same order as they appear in the picklist.**

| Profit | 304,325 |
|---|---|
| **Disallowed items added back** | |
| ▼ | |
| ▼ | |
| ▼ | |
| ▼ | |
| ▼ | |
| ▼ | |
| Total added back | |
| **Allowed items deducted** | |
| ▼ | |
| Adjusted trading profits | |

**Drop-down list 1:**

Accounting fee / Legal costs for tax appeal / Redecoration / Installation / Depreciation / Donation to local charity / Cost of Easter eggs / Cost of wine / Customer entertainment

**Drop-down list 2:**

Depreciation / Capital allowances

(b) **For each of the following items, pick the correct treatment in relation to the computation of the taxable profit.**

| | |
|---|---|
| Private use of vehicle by partner | ▼ |
| Gain on the sale of land | ▼ |
| Staff party £30 per head | ▼ |
| Purchase of new motor vehicle | ▼ |

**Drop-down list:**

Allowed
Disallowed and add back
Disallowed and deduct

## Task 2 (14 marks)

Barraden Ltd has the following fixed asset information for the nine month period ended 31 January 2015:

| Balances brought forward as at 1 May 2014 | £ |
|---|---|
| General pool | 278,520 |
| Managing Director's car<br>C02 emissions of 191 g/km<br>30% private use | 24,800 |

| Additions | £ |
|---|---|
| Plant | 369,300 |
| Delivery lorry | 35,600 |
| Sales Director's car<br>C02 emissions of 115 g/km<br>15% private use | 20,300 |

Due to the sudden loss of a major order, the company had to cease trading on 31 March 2015. On 31 March 2015, the proceeds or market value for each pool were:

| | £ |
|---|---|
| General plant – proceeds | 282,000 |
| Managing Director's car retained at market value | 19,800 |
| Sales Director's car – proceeds | 15,400 |

**Calculate the capital allowances for the period ended 31 January 2015 and the final period ended 31 March 2015.**

| | | | | |
|---|---|---|---|---|
| | | | | |
| | | | | |
| | | | | |
| | | | | |
| | | | | |
| | | | | |
| | | | | |
| | | | | |
| | | | | |
| | | | | |
| | | | | |
| | | | | |

## Task 3 (12 marks)

Gordon commenced trading on 1 December 2012. His taxable profits have been agreed as follows:

| | |
|---|---|
| Period ended 30 June 2013 | £50,750 |
| Year ended 30 June 2014 | £106,800 |
| Year ended 30 June 2015 | £77,400 |

**Calculate the taxable profits and state the tax year and basis period for the first three tax years of trading. Insert the tax year dates as XXXX/XX (eg 2013/14) and the basis period dates as XX/XX/XXXX (eg 01/12/2012).**

| | Tax year<br>XXXX / XX | Basis period<br>XX/XX/XXXX – XX/XX/XXXX | Profit<br>£ |
|---|---|---|---|
| First year | ☐ / ☐ | ☐ – ☐ | ☐ |
| Second year | ☐ / ☐ | ☐ – ☐ | ☐ |
| Third year | ☐ , / ☐ | ☐ – ☐ | ☐ |

## Task 4 (12 marks)

Reece Ltd made up accounts for the 18 month period ended 31 January 2015. The following details have been extracted from the accounts:

The company had made a capital gain of £14,960 in January 2014 on the sale of a factory. It had also made a capital gain of £8,060 in November 2014 on the sale of shares. Its trading profits for the period amounted to £188,640.

(a) **State the amount taken into account in each of the following accounting periods. If your answer is zero, enter 0.**

| | First accounting period<br>£ | Second accounting period<br>£ |
|---|---|---|
| Capital gains | | |
| Trading profits | | |

(b) **Tick the correct box to show whether the following statement is True or False:**

| | True | False |
|---|---|---|
| Total taxable profits includes all dividends received from other companies. | ☐ | ☐ |

A company has the following information for the year ended 31 March 2015:

- Taxable total profits are £180,000.
- Dividends received (net) are £10,800.
- The company has two associated companies.

(c) **Calculate the marginal relief that would apply.**

| Marginal relief for Finance Year 2014 | £ |
|---|---|
| 1/400 × [            ] – [            ] × [          ]/[          ] | [            ] |

## Task 5 (4 marks)

The details of the profits for two self-employed musicians for 2014/15 are as follows:

| Names | Profit £ |
|---|---|
| Jonathan | 24,300 |
| Charlotte | 58,060 |

**Calculate the Class 4 National Insurance Contributions for both Jonathan and Charlotte for 2014/15. Your answer should be to the nearest penny. If your answer is zero, enter 0.**

| Names | Class 4 at 9% £ | Class 4 at 2% £ |
|---|---|---|
| Jonathan | | |
| Charlotte | | |

## Task 6 (6 marks)

Daffodil Ltd has the following results from the last two years of trading.

| Year ended | 31 January 2015 £ | 31 January 2014 £ |
|---|---|---|
| Trading (loss)/profit | (37,400) | 8,500 |
| Chargeable gain/(loss) | 4,000 | (2,900) |
| Gross interest received | 1,200 | 1,200 |
| Gift aid (qualifying charitable donation) | 600 | 600 |

Daffodil Ltd has a policy of always claiming relief for their losses as soon as possible.

**Enter the relevant amounts in the box below to show how Daffodil Ltd would claim for their trading loss. If your answer is zero, enter 0.**

| | £ |
|---|---|
| How much trading loss relief can be claimed against income in the year ended 31 January 2015? | |
| How much trading loss relief can be claimed against income in the year ended 31 January 2014? | |
| How much trading loss relief can be carried forward to the year ended 31 January 2016? | |
| How much gift aid (qualifying charitable donation) can be carried forward to the year ended 31 January 2016? | |
| How much capital loss can be carried forward to the year ended 31 January 2016? | |

## Task 7 (10 marks)

Jolene is one of your clients. She has several hairdressing shops and over the past few years, you have agreed her tax liabilities as:

| Tax year | £ |
|---|---|
| 2011/12 | 22,450 |
| 2012/13 | 28,600 |
| 2013/14 | 33,900 |
| 2014/15 | 36,750 |

She has told you that she does not understand when she needs to pay her tax to HMRC and she is worried that if she misses important dates, she will be heavily fined by HMRC.

**In the box below you need to respond to Jolene's query by explaining:**

(a) **the amount and date of each payment Jolene needs to make for the calendar year of 2014.**

(b) **the penalties and/or interest that she would incur if she was late in paying her tax on the due dates.**

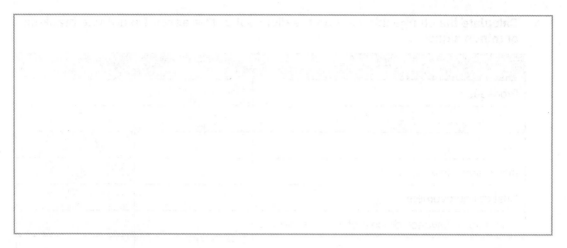

## Task 8 (6 marks)

The following details have been extracted from the accounts and tax computations of Sparkle Ltd for the year ended 31 March 2015:

- Sparkle Ltd had one associated company
- the profit for the year was £1,330,500
- net dividends received were £94,500

**Complete the relevant boxes on the following return for each of the above.**

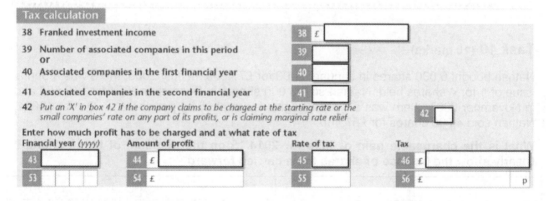

## Task 9 (8 marks)

Richie Ltd sold an asset in July 2014 for £195,750. This asset had been bought in January 1998 for £37,820 and in October 2005, £19,000 had been spent on improving it.

Indexation factors are:

| | |
|---|---|
| January 1998 to October 2005 | 0.212 |
| January 1998 to July 2014 | 0.608 |
| October 2005 to July 2014 | 0.326 |

(a) **Calculate the chargeable gain on the disposal of this asset. Do not use brackets or minus signs.**

|  | £ | £ |
|---|---|---|
| Proceeds |  |  |
|  |  |  |
| Cost |  |  |
| Indexation allowance on cost |  |  |
| Cost of improvement |  |  |
| Indexation allowance on cost of improvement |  |  |
| Gain |  |  |

(b) **Tick to show if the following statements are True or False.**

|  | True | False |
|---|---|---|
| Capital gains tax is not payable by limited companies. | ☐ | ☐ |
| The gift of an asset is not treated as a chargeable disposal. | ☐ | ☐ |

## Task 10 (10 marks)

Nathan bought 6,000 shares in January 2000 for £77,800. In July 2003, there was a bonus issue of 1 for 4 shares held. Nathan sold 3,000 shares in December 2004 for £40,500 and in November 2007, there was a 1 for 10 rights issue at £5.50 per share. In October 2014, Nathan sold 4,000 shares for £57,400.

**What is the chargeable gain or loss for 2014/15 on the disposal of these shares? Clearly show the balance of shares to be carried forward.**

|  |  |  |  |
|---|---|---|---|
|  |  |  |  |
|  |  |  |  |
|  |  |  |  |
|  |  |  |  |
|  |  |  |  |
|  |  |  |  |
|  |  |  |  |
|  |  |  |  |
|  |  |  |  |
|  |  |  |  |

| | | | |
|---|---|---|---|
| | | | |
| | | | |
| | | | |

.......................................................................................

## Task 11 (6 marks)

Three taxpayers sold similar assets during 2014/15 and each made a capital gain, after deducting their annual exemption (annual exempt amount), of £21,500. In the table below, the total of their other taxable income is shown.

**Show the amount of capital gain that would be chargeable under each of the two rates capital gains tax (CGT). You must enter 0 if your answer is zero.**

| Taxpayer | Other income (£) | Chargeable capital gain (£) | |
|---|---|---|---|
| | | 18% CGT rate | 28% CGT rate |
| Precious | 14,300 | | |
| Rosie | 29,400 | | |
| Gavin | 57,900 | | |

.......................................................................................

# AAT AQ2013
# SAMPLE ASSESSMENT
# BUSINESS TAX

# ANSWERS

# Business Tax AAT (AQ2013) sample assessment

## Task 1 (12 marks)

(a) **Complete the computation. Do not use minus signs or brackets to show negative figures.**

| Profit | | 304,325 |
|---|---|---|
| **Disallowed items added back** | | |
| Legal costs for tax appeal | ▼ | 8,690 |
| Installation | ▼ | 14,130 |
| Depreciation | ▼ | 148,860 |
| Cost of Easter eggs | ▼ | 800 |
| Cost of wine | ▼ | 1,400 |
| Customer entertainment | ▼ | 2,450 |
| Total added back | | 176,330 |
| **Allowed items deducted** | | |
| Capital allowances | ▼ | 142,950 |
| Adjusted trading profits | | 337,705 |

(b) **For each of the following items, pick the correct treatment in relation to the computation of the taxable profit.**

| | |
|---|---|
| Private use of vehicle by partner | Disallowed and add back ▼ |
| Gain on the sale of land | Disallowed and deduct ▼ |
| Staff party £30 per head | Allowed ▼ |
| Purchase of new motor vehicle | Disallowed and add back ▼ |

## Task 2 (14 marks)

| Period ended 31 January 2015 | | General Pool £ | Car Pool £ | Allow £ |
|---|---|---|---|---|
| B/fwd | | 278,520 | 24,800 | |
| Non AIA additions | | 20,300 | | |
| | | 298,820 | | |
| AIA additions: | | | | |
| Plant | 369,300 | | | |
| Lorry | 35,600 | | | |
| | 404,900 | | | |
| AIA: £500,000 × 9/12 | 375,000 | 29,900 | | 375,000 |
| | | 328,720 | 24,800 | |
| WDA 18% × 9/12 | | 44,377 | | 44,377 |
| WDA 8% × 9/12 | | | 1,488 | 1,488 |
| c/f | | 284,343 | 23,312 | **420,865** |
| Period ended | | | | |
| 31 March 2015 | | | | |
| Sales proceeds/value | | 297,400 | 19,800 | |
| Balancing allowance | | | 3,512 | 3,512 |
| Balancing charge | | 13,057 | | (13,057) |
| | | | | **(9,545)** |

## Task 3 (12 marks)

Gordon commenced trading on 1 December 2012. His taxable profits have been agreed as follows:

| | |
|---|---|
| Period ended 30 June 2013 | £50,750 |
| Year ended 30 June 2014 | £106,800 |
| Year ended 30 June 2015 | £77,400 |

**Calculate the taxable profits and state the tax year and basis period for the first three tax years of trading. Insert the tax year dates as XXXX/XX (eg 2013/14) and the basis period dates as XX/XX/XXXX (eg 01/12/2012).**

| | Tax year YYYY / YY | Basis period XX/XX/XXXX - XX/XX/XXXX | Profit £ |
|---|---|---|---|
| First year | 2012 / 13 | 01/12/2012 – 05/04/2013 | 29,000 |
| Second year | 2013 / 14 | 01/12/2012 – 30/11/2013 | 95,250 |
| Third year | 2014 / 15 | 01/07/2013 – 30/06/2014 | 106,800 |

## Task 4 (12 marks)

Reece Ltd made up accounts for the 18 month period ended 31 January 2015. The following details have been extracted from the accounts:

The company had made a capital gain of £14,960 in January 2014 on the sale of a factory. It had also made a capital gain of £8,060 in November 2014 on the sale of shares. Its trading profits for the period amounted to £188,640.

(a) **State the amount taken into account in each of the following accounting periods. If your answer is zero, enter 0.**

| | First accounting period £ | Second accounting period £ |
|---|---|---|
| Capital gains | 14,960 | 8,060 |
| Trading profits | 125,760 | 62,880 |

(b) **Tick the correct box to show whether the following statement is True or False:**

| | True | False |
|---|---|---|
| Total taxable profits includes all dividends received from other companies. | ☐ | ✓ |

A company has the following information for the year ended 31 March 2015:

- Taxable total profits are £180,000.
- Dividends received (net) are £10,800.
- The company has two associated companies.

(c) **Calculate the marginal relief that would apply.**

| Marginal relief for Finance Year 2014 | £ |
|---|---|
| 1/400 × [ 500,000 ] − [ 192,000 ] × $\dfrac{180,000}{192,000}$ | 722 |

## Task 5 (4 marks)

The details of the profits for two self-employed musicians for 2014/15 are as follows:

| Names | Profit £ |
|---|---|
| Jonathan | 24,300 |
| Charlotte | 58,060 |

Calculate the Class 4 National Insurance Contributions for both Jonathan and Charlotte for 2014/15. Your answer should be to the nearest penny. If your answer is zero, enter 0.

| Names | Class 4 at 9% £ | Class 4 at 2% £ |
|---|---|---|
| Jonathan | 1,470.96 | 0 |
| Charlotte | 3,051.81 | 323.90 |

## Task 6 (6 marks)

Daffodil Ltd has the following results from the last two years of trading.

| Year ended | 31 January 2015 £ | 31 January 2014 £ |
|---|---|---|
| Trading (loss)/profit | (37,400) | 8,500 |
| Chargeable gain/(loss) | 4,000 | (2,900) |
| Gross interest received | 1,200 | 1,200 |
| Gift aid (qualifying charitable donation) | 600 | 600 |

Daffodil Ltd has a policy of always claiming relief for their losses as soon as possible.

**Enter the relevant amounts in the box below to show how Daffodil Ltd would claim for their trading loss. If your answer is zero, enter 0.**

| | £ |
|---|---|
| How much trading loss relief can be claimed against income in the year ended 31 January 2015? | 2,300 |
| How much trading loss relief can be claimed against income in the year ended 31 January 2014? | 9,700 |
| How much trading loss relief can be carried forward to the year ended 31 January 2016? | 25,400 |
| How much gift aid (qualifying charitable donation) can be carried forward to the year ended 31 January 2016? | 0 |
| How much capital loss can be carried forward to the year ended 31 January 2016? | 0 |

## Task 7 (10 marks)

Jolene is one of your clients. She has several hairdressing shops and over the past few years, you have agreed her tax liabilities as:

| Tax year | £ |
| --- | --- |
| 2011/12 | 22,450 |
| 2012/13 | 28,600 |
| 2013/14 | 33,900 |
| 2014/15 | 36,750 |

She has told you that she does not understand when she needs to pay her tax to HMRC and she is worried that if she misses important dates, she will be heavily fined by HMRC.

**In the box below you need to respond to Jolene's query by explaining:**

(a) **the amount and date of each payment Jolene needs to make for the calendar year of 2014.**

(b) **the penalties and/or interest that she would incur if she was late in paying her tax on the due dates.**

| (a) | Dates | Working | £ |
| --- | --- | --- | --- |
| | 31 January 2014 | (28,600 – 22,450) + (28,600/2) | 20,450 |
| | 31 July 2014 | 28,600/2 | 14,300 |

(b) Penalties and interest:

Interest is payable on all late payments. The interest is charged from the due date of payment to the actual date of payment.

Penalties are also due on late balancing payments. This is equal to 5% of the tax not paid if late by 30 days. Two further penalties are imposed at 5% each for tax remaining unpaid 6 months and 12 months after the due date.

## Task 8 (6 marks)

The following details have been extracted from the accounts and tax computations of Sparkle Ltd for the year ended 31 March 2015:

- Sparkle Ltd had one associated company.
- The profit for the year was £1,330,500.
- Net dividends received were £94,500.

**Complete the relevant boxes on the following return for each of the above.**

| Tax calculation | | |
|---|---|---|
| 38 Franked investment income | 38 £ | 105,000 |
| 39 Number of associated companies in this period<br>or | 39 | 1 |
| 40 Associated companies in the first financial year | 40 | |
| 41 Associated companies in the second financial year | 41 | |
| 42 Put an 'X' in box 42 if the company claims to be charged at the starting rate or the small companies' rate on any part of its profits, or is claiming marginal rate relief | 42 | |

Enter how much profit has to be charged and at what rate of tax

| Financial year (yyyy) | Amount of profit | Rate of tax | Tax |
|---|---|---|---|
| 43 2014 | 44 £ 1,330,500 | 45 21% | 46 £ 279,405 |
| 53 | 54 £ | 55 | 56 £    p |

## Task 9 (8 marks)

Richie Ltd sold an asset in July 2014 for £195,750. This asset had been bought in January 1998 for £37,820 and in October 2005, £19,000 had been spent on improving it.

Indexation factors are:

| | |
|---|---|
| January 1998 to October 2005 | 0.212 |
| January 1998 to July 2014 | 0.608 |
| October 2005 to July 2014 | 0.326 |

(a) **Calculate the chargeable gain on the disposal of this asset. Do not use brackets or minus signs.**

| | £ | £ |
|---|---|---|
| Proceeds | | 195,750 |
| | | |
| Cost | 37,820 | |
| Indexation allowance on cost | 22,995 | |
| Cost of improvement | 19,000 | |
| Indexation allowance on cost of improvement | 6,194 | |
| Gain | | 109,741 |

(b) **Tick to show if the following statements are True or False.**

| | True | False |
|---|---|---|
| Capital gains tax is not payable by limited companies. | ✓ | |
| The gift of an asset is not treated as a chargeable disposal | | ✓ |

## Task 10 (10 marks)

Nathan bought 6,000 shares in January 2000 for £77,800. In July 2003, there was a bonus issue of 1 for 4 shares held. Nathan sold 3,000 shares in December 2004 for £40,500 and in November 2007, there was a 1 for 10 rights issue at £5.50 per share. In October 2014, Nathan sold 4,000 shares for £57,400.

**What is the chargeable gain or loss for 2014/15 on the disposal of these shares? Clearly show the balance of shares to be carried forward.**

|  |  | No of Shares | Cost (£) |
| --- | --- | --- | --- |
| January 2000 | Purchase | 6,000 | 77,800 |
| July 2003 | Bonus issue | 1,500 | 0 |
|  |  | 7,500 | 77,800 |
| December 2004 | Disposal | (3,000) | (31,120) |
|  |  | 4,500 | 46,680 |
| November 2007 | Rights issue | 450 | 2,475 |
|  |  | 4,950 | 49,155 |
| October 2014 | Disposal | (4,000) | (39,721) |
|  |  | 950 | 9,434 |
|  |  |  |  |
|  | Proceeds | 57,400 |  |
|  | Cost | 39,721 |  |
|  | Gain | 17,679 |  |

## Task 11 (6 marks)

Three taxpayers sold similar assets during 2014/15 and each made a capital gain, after deducting their annual exemption (annual exempt amount), of £21,500. In the table below, the total of their other taxable income is shown.

**Show the amount of capital gain that would be chargeable under each of the two rates capital gains tax (CGT). You must enter 0 if your answer is zero.**

| Taxpayer | Other income (£) | Chargeable capital gain (£) | |
|---|---|---|---|
| | | 18% CGT rate | 28% CGT rate |
| Precious | 14,300 | 17,565 | 3,935 |
| Rosie | 29,400 | 2,465 | 19,035 |
| Gavin | 57,900 | 0 | 21,500 |

# BPP PRACTICE ASSESSMENT 1
# BUSINESS TAX

**Time allowed: 2 hours**

# Taxation Data

## Taxation tables for Business Tax – 2014/15

**Note that 'TAXATION DATA 1' and 'TAXATION DATA 2' shown below will be available as pop up windows throughout your live assessment.**

### TAXATION DATA 1

| | |
|---|---:|
| *Capital allowances* | |
| Annual investment allowance | |
| From 1 January 2013 | £250,000 |
| From 1/6 April 2014 | £500,000 |
| Plant and machinery writing down allowance | 18% |
| Motor cars | |
| $CO_2$ emissions up to 95g/km | 100% |
| $CO_2$ emissions between 96g/km and 130g/km | 18% |
| $CO_2$ emissions over 130g/km | 8% |
| Energy efficient and water saving plant | |
| First year allowance | 100% |
| *Capital gains* | |
| Annual exempt amount | £11,000 |
| Standard rate | 18% |
| Higher rate (applicable over £31,865) | 28% |
| Entrepreneurs' relief rate | 10% |
| Entrepreneurs' relief limit | £10,000,000 |
| *National insurance rates* | |
| Class 2 contributions: | £2.75 per week |
| Small earnings exception | £5,885 p.a. |
| Class 4 contributions: | |
| Main rate | 9% |
| Additional rate | 2% |
| Lower profits limit | £7,956 |
| Upper profits limit | £41,865 |

### TAXATION DATA 2

| *Corporation tax* | | |
|---|---:|---:|
| *Financial year* | *2014* | *2013* |
| Small profits rate | 20% | 20% |
| Marginal relief: | | |
| Lower limit | £300,000 | £300,000 |
| Upper limit | £1,500,000 | £1,500,000 |
| Standard fraction | 1/400 | 3/400 |
| Main rate | 21% | 23% |

Marginal relief formula: Fraction $\times$ (U–A) $\times$
N/A

# Business Tax BPP practice assessment 1

## Task 1

The income statement for George Checkers shows the following:

|  | £ | £ |
|---|---|---|
| Gross profit |  | 396,550 |
| General expenses (see notes below) | 85,480 |  |
| Irrecoverable debts (see notes below) | 585 |  |
| Motor expenses (see notes below) | 7,880 |  |
| Wages and salaries | 54,455 |  |
| Depreciation charge | 21,080 |  |
|  |  | (169,480) |
| Profit for the year |  | 227,070 |

Notes include:

| General expenses include: | £ |
|---|---|
| Gifts to customers – Christmas cakes costing £4.50 each | 1,350 |
| Building a new wall around car park | 2,200 |

| Irrecoverable debts are made up of: | £ |
|---|---|
| Trade debts written-off | 350 |
| Increase in general provision | 400 |
| Trade debts recovered | (165) |
|  | 585 |

| Motor expenses are made up of: | Private usage % | Annual expense £ |
|---|---|---|
| George | 25 | 6,600 |
| Salesman | 20 | 1,280 |
| Capital allowances computed to be: |  | £15,000 |

(a) **Complete the computation provided below. Fill in all unshaded boxes. Do not use minus signs or brackets to show negative numbers.**

|  | £ |
|---|---|
| Profit for the year per accounts |  |
| Disallowed items added back |  |
| [A] ▼ |  |
| [B] ▼ |  |
| [C] ▼ |  |
| [D] ▼ |  |
| [E] ▼ |  |
| Total to add back |  |
| Allowed items deducted |  |
| [F] ▼ |  |
| Adjusted trading profits |  |

| **Picklist for A to E** *(please keep them in order)* |
|---|
| gifts to customers – cakes |
| new wall |
| trade debts written-off |
| increase in general provision |
| private motor expenses – George |
| private motor expenses – salesman |
| depreciation charge |
| **Picklist for F** |
| trade debts recovered |
| capital allowances |

(b) **For the following items, tick the correct treatment when computing the adjusted trading profits:**

| | Allowed | Disallowed – add back | Disallowed – deduct |
|---|---|---|---|
| Purchase of raw materials | ☐ | ☐ | ☐ |
| Private use of vehicle by an employee | ☐ | ☐ | ☐ |
| Purchase of delivery van | ☐ | ☐ | ☐ |
| Interest received on business bank account | ☐ | ☐ | ☐ |

## Task 2

Mr Wish commenced trade on 1 July 2014. He made up his first set of accounts for six months to 31 December 2014 and yearly from then on.

The following fixed asset information is available for his first 18 months of trade:

| Date | Additions | Cost (£) |
|---|---|---|
| 1 July 14 | New plant and machinery. | 280,400 |
| 15 July 14 | A car with $CO_2$ emissions of 120g/km. Mr Wish used this car 75% of the time for business purposes. | 16,000 |
| 2 Mar 15 | A car with $CO_2$ emissions of 190g/km. This car is used 20% of the time by a salesman for private purposes. | 28,000 |
| 2 July 15 | A new car for Mr Wish with $CO_2$ emissions of 90g/km. Mr Wish used this car 75% of the time for business purposes. | 17,500 |

| Date | Disposals | Proceeds (£) |
|---|---|---|
| 15 Dec 14 | Plant purchased for £32,000. | 18,000 |
| 1 July 15 | Mr Wish's car bought on 15 July 14. | 15,300 |

**Calculate the capital allowances for Mr Wish for the six month period ended 31 December 2014 and the year ended 31 December 2015. Show the balances to carry forward to the next accounting period.**

|  | £ | £ | £ | £ | £ | £ | £ |
|---|---|---|---|---|---|---|---|
|  |  |  |  |  |  |  |  |
|  |  |  |  |  |  |  |  |
|  |  |  |  |  |  |  |  |
|  |  |  |  |  |  |  |  |
|  |  |  |  |  |  |  |  |
|  |  |  |  |  |  |  |  |
|  |  |  |  |  |  |  |  |
|  |  |  |  |  |  |  |  |
|  |  |  |  |  |  |  |  |
|  |  |  |  |  |  |  |  |
|  |  |  |  |  |  |  |  |
|  |  |  |  |  |  |  |  |
|  |  |  |  |  |  |  |  |
|  |  |  |  |  |  |  |  |
|  |  |  |  |  |  |  |  |
|  |  |  |  |  |  |  |  |
|  |  |  |  |  |  |  |  |
|  |  |  |  |  |  |  |  |
|  |  |  |  |  |  |  |  |
|  |  |  |  |  |  |  |  |
|  |  |  |  |  |  |  |  |
|  |  |  |  |  |  |  |  |
|  |  |  |  |  |  |  |  |

## Task 3

(a)  Jude and Kelly have been in partnership for many years making up accounts to 30 September each year. They share profits 3:1 respectively.

On 1 July 2014, Liam joined the partnership. It was agreed that Liam would be paid a salary of £6,000 per year and that profits would be shared 2:2:1 for Jude, Kelly and Liam.

For the year ended 30 September 2014, the partnership trading profit was £54,000.

**Show the division of profits between the partners for the year ended 30 September 2014 in the table below. Fill in all unshaded boxes and add a 0 (zero) if necessary.**

|  | Jude | Kelly | Liam |
|---|---|---|---|
| (insert dates as: xx/xx/xxxx) | £ | £ | £ |
| Period to: | | | |
|  | | | |
| Division of profits | | | |
| Period to: | | | |
|  | | | |
| Salary | | | |
| Division of profits | | | |
| Total profit for y/e 30/09/2014 | | | |

(b)  The following accounts have been prepared for a sole trader:

|  | £ |
|---|---|
| Year ended 30 June 2014 | 45,000 |
| Year ended 30 June 2015 | 42,000 |
| Period to 30 November 2015 | 15,000 |

The trade ceased on 30 November 2015 and overlap profits from commencement were £9,500.

(1)  **The penultimate tax year is: (insert as (xxxx/xx)**

（　　　　　　　）

(2)  **The final tax year is: (insert as (xxxx/xx)**

（　　　　　　　）

(3) **The profits for the penultimate year of trade are:**

£ [                    ]

(4) **The profits for the final year of trade are:**

£ [                    ]

........................................................................................

## Task 4

(a) A company made up accounts to 31 December 2013. It decides to make up its next set of accounts to 31 March 2015.

**Identify how the company will deal with its capital allowances in the long period of account. Tick ONE box.**

|  | ✓ |
| --- | --- |
| One computation from 1 January 2014 to 31 March 2015 |  |
| Two computations: one from 1 January 2014 to 31 March 2014 and one from 1 April 2014 to 31 March 2015 |  |
| Two computations: one from 1 January 2014 to 31 December 2014 and one from 1 January 2015 to 31 March 2015 |  |
| It can deal with the computation for whatever period the company chooses |  |

(b) Abbey Ltd has the following information for the year ended 31 March 2015.

The adjusted trading profit, after deducting capital allowances, was £620,843.

The company sold a piece of investment land in December 2014 realising a gain of £67,817.

Abbey Ltd has one wholly owned subsidiary.

(1) **Abbey Ltd's taxable total profits are:**

£ [                    ]

(2) **The applicable upper limit is:**

£ [                    ]

**and the applicable lower limit is:**

£ [                    ]

(3) **The corporation tax payable for the year ended 31 March 2015 is:**

£ [                    ]

(4)  **The due date for payment is: (insert as (xx/xx/xxxx)**

[   ]

(c)  T Ltd, a large company, has a corporation tax liability of £600,000 in respect of its accounting year ended 31 December 2014

**Identify the date the company will be required to pay its FINAL instalment of the liability. Tick ONE box.**

|  | ✓ |
|---|---|
| 14 October 2014 |  |
| 14 January 2015 |  |
| 14 April 2015 |  |
| 1 October 2015 |  |

---

## Task 5

Crystal is a sole trader who has taxable trading profits of £91,750 for the year ended 31 December 2014.

**Crystal's Class 2 NIC liability for 2014/15 is: (show your answer to the nearest penny)**

£ [       ] • [    ]

**Crystal's Class 4 NIC liability for 2014/15 is: (show your answer to the nearest penny)**

£ [       ] • [    ]

Pearl is a sole trader who has taxable trading profits of £27,300 for the year ended 31 December 2014.

**Pearl's Class 2 NIC liability for 2014/15 is: (show your answer to the nearest penny)**

£ [       ] • [    ]

**Pearl's Class 4 NIC liability for 2014/15 is: (show your answer to the nearest penny)**

£ [       ] • [    ]

---

## Task 6

(a) **Identify whether the following statements are True or False.**

| | True ✓ | False ✓ |
|---|---|---|
| A sole trader must make a claim to set a loss made in 2014/15 against total income in 2014/15 before making a claim to set the loss against total income in 2013/14 | | |
| A sole trader can carry trade losses forward and choose the best year to use them | | |
| A sole trader can only offset trading losses brought forward against profits of the same trade | | |

(b) A limited company makes a trading loss of £47,300 in its year ended 31 March 2015. It has also made a chargeable gain of £52,350 in the same period, and has capital losses brought forward of £5,200. The company has a policy of claiming relief for its losses as soon as possible.

    (1) **The amount of trading loss that can be claimed against profits in year ended 31 March 2015 is:**

       £ [                    ]

    (2) **The amount of trading loss that can be carried forward to the year ended 31 March 2016 is:**

       £ [                    ]

......................................................................................................

## Task 7

Mina is a client of yours. She has income tax and Class 4 national insurance contributions payable for 2014/15 of £4,225, but was not required to make any payments on account for this tax year.

Mina is looking for advice about when she needs to pay this tax. She has also advised you that she accidentally forgot to include quite a substantial trading invoice in her tax return for 2013/14, and is wondering what to do about this and whether she might incur a penalty.

**In the box below respond to Mina's query by explaining:**

(a) **when she should pay the 2014/15 income tax and Class 4 NIC**

(b) **how much each payment on account will be for 2015/16 and when these should be paid**

(c) **when the balancing payment 2015/16 would be due and how this is calculated**

(d) **the penalty that she may incur for a careless (non deliberate) error on her return, and what she could do to try and reduce this penalty**

## Task 8

**Complete the following extract from the tax return for Spire Ltd for the year ended 31 March 2015 using the information below.**

The adjusted trading profit, after deducting capital allowances was £865,000.

The company sold a piece of investment land in August 2014 realising a gain of £73,500.

Spire Ltd has one associated company.

Dividends of £108,000 (net) were received from a non associated company on 31 December 2014.

Page 2

# Company tax calculation

## Turnover

| | | |
|---|---|---|
| 1 | Total turnover from trade or profession | **1** £ |

## Income

| | | |
|---|---|---|
| 3 | Trading and professional profits | **3** £ |
| 4 | Trading losses brought forward claimed against profits | **4** £ |
| | | *box 3 minus box 4* |
| 5 | Net trading and professional profits | **5** £ |
| 6 | Bank, building society or other interest, and profits and gains from non-trading loan relationships | **6** £ |
| 11 | Income from UK land and buildings | **11** £ |
| 14 | Annual profits and gains not falling under any other heading | **14** £ |

## Chargeable gains

| | | |
|---|---|---|
| 16 | Gross chargeable gains | **16** £ |
| 17 | Allowable losses including losses brought forward | **17** £ |
| | | *box 16 minus box 17* |
| 18 | Net chargeable gains | **18** £ |
| | | *sum of boxes 5, 6, 11, 14 & 18* |
| **21** | **Profits before other deductions and reliefs** | **21** £ |

## Deductions and Reliefs

| | | |
|---|---|---|
| 24 | Management expenses under S75 ICTA 1988 | **24** £ |
| 30 | Trading losses of this or a later accounting period under S393A ICTA 1988 | **30** £ |
| 31 | Put an 'X' in box 31 if amounts carried back from later accounting periods are included in box 30 | **31** |
| 32 | Non-trade capital allowances | **32** £ |
| 35 | Charges paid | **35** £ |
| | | *box 21 minus boxes 24, 30, 32 and 35* |
| **37** | **Taxable total profits** | **37** £ |

## Tax calculation

| | | |
|---|---|---|
| 38 | Franked investment income | **38** £ |
| 39 | Number of associated companies in this period or | **39** |
| 40 | Associated companies in the first financial year | **40** |
| 41 | Associated companies in the second financial year | **41** |
| 42 | Put an 'X' in box 42 if the company claims to be charged at the starting rate or the small companies' rate on any part of its profits, or is claiming marginal rate relief | **42** |

Enter how much profit has to be charged and at what rate of tax

| Financial year (yyyy) | Amount of profit | Rate of tax | Tax |
|---|---|---|---|
| **43** | **44** £ | **45** | **46** £   p |
| **53** | **54** £ | **55** | **56** £   p |
| | | | *total of boxes 46 and 56* |

| | | |
|---|---|---|
| 63 | Corporation tax | **63** £   p |
| 64 | Marginal rate relief | **64** £   p |
| 65 | Corporation tax net of marginal rate relief | **65** £   p |
| 66 | Underlying rate of corporation tax | **66** • % |
| 67 | Profits matched with non-corporate distributions | **67** |
| 68 | Tax at non-corporate distributions rate | **68** £   p |
| 69 | Tax at underlying rate on remaining profits | **69** £   p |
| | | *See note for box 70 in CT600 Guide* |
| **70** | **Corporation tax chargeable** | **70** £   p |

CT600 (Short) (2008) Version 2

151

## Task 9

(a) **For the following disposals, tick if it would be exempt or chargeable:**

|  | Exempt | Chargeable |
|---|---|---|
| Disposal of a vintage car worth £40,000 | ☐ | ☐ |
| Gift of land to a charity | ☐ | ☐ |
| Gift of jewellery on the taxpayer's death | ☐ | ☐ |

(b) Nick bought a five-acre plot of land for £50,000. He sold three acres of the land at auction for £105,000. He had spent £2,500 installing drainage on the three acres which he sold. His disposal costs were £1,500. The market value of the remaining two acres at the date of sale was £45,000.

**Calculate the chargeable gain on the disposal of the three acres of land using the table below (do not use brackets or minus signs).**

|  | £ |
|---|---|
| Gross proceeds | |
| Costs of disposal | |
| Net proceeds | |
| Cost | |
| Enhancement expenditure | |
| Chargeable gain | |

## Task 10

In May 2014, Green Ltd sold 4,000 of the shares it held in Blue Ltd for £130,000. These shares had been acquired as follows:

|  | No of shares | £ |
|---|---|---|
| April 1989 | 2,000 | 25,000 |
| June 1994 | 2,000 | 35,000 |
| July 1997 – bonus issue | 1 for 10 | |
| September 2002 – rights issue | 1 for 5 | £10 per share |

*Indexation factors:*

| | |
|---|---|
| April 1989 to June 1994 | 0.266 |
| June 1994 to July 1997 | 0.088 |
| June 1994 to September 2002 | 0.227 |
| July 1997 to September 2002 | 0.128 |
| September 2002 to May 2014 | 0.441 |

**Calculate the chargeable gain on the sale of these shares in May 2014.**

| | | | |
|---|---|---|---|
| | | | |
| | | | |
| | | | |
| | | | |
| | | | |
| | | | |
| | | | |
| | | | |
| | | | |
| | | | |
| | | | |
| | | | |
| | | | |
| | | | |
| | | | |
| | | | |
| | | | |
| | | | |
| | | | |
| | | | |
| | | | |
| | | | |

## Task 11

(a) **Identify whether the following statements are True or False.**

|  | True ✓ | False ✓ |
|---|---|---|
| If an individual has allowable capital losses brought forward, these are only used to bring gains down to the annual exempt amount. | | |
| Allowable capital losses of the current year can be restricted to bring the net current year gains down to the annual exempt amount. | | |
| Allowable capital losses can be carried back against gains in the previous 12 month period. | | |

(b) In November 2014, Cowley Ltd sold its factory for £260,000. It bought the factory in December 2006 for £150,000. In March 2014, it bought a replacement factory for £230,000 and claimed rollover relief. The indexation factor between December 2006 to November 2014 is 0.277.

(1) **The gain on the disposal is:**

£ [          ]

(2) **The gain immediately chargeable is:**

£ [          ]

(3) **The gain rolled-over:**

£ [          ]

# BPP PRACTICE ASSESSMENT 1
# BUSINESS TAX

# ANSWERS

# Business Tax BPP practice assessment 1

## Task 1

(a) **Complete the computation provided below. Fill in all unshaded boxes. Do not use minus signs or brackets to show negative numbers.**

|  | £ |
|---|---|
| Profit for the year per accounts | 227,070 |
| Disallowed items added back |  |
| gifts to customers – cakes | 1,350 |
| new wall | 2,200 |
| increase in general provision | 400 |
| private motor expenses – George | 1,650 |
| depreciation charge | 21,080 |
| Total to add back | 26,680 |
| Allowed items deducted |  |
| Capital allowances | 15,000 |
| Adjusted trading profits | 238,750 |

(b) **For the following items, tick the correct treatment when computing the adjusted trading profits.**

|  | Allowed | Disallowed – add back | Disallowed – deduct |
|---|---|---|---|
| Purchase of raw materials | ✓ |  |  |
| Private use of vehicle by an employee | ✓ |  |  |
| Purchase of delivery van |  | ✓ |  |
| Interest received on business bank account |  |  | ✓ |

## Task 2

Calculate the capital allowances for Mr Wish for the six month period ended 31 December 2014 and the year ended 31 December 2015. Show the balances to carry forward to the next accounting period.

| | AIA | Main pool | Special rate pool | Owner's car | | Allowances |
|---|---|---|---|---|---|---|
| | £ | £ | £ | £ | | £ |
| **Period to 31 Dec 14** | | | | | | |
| *AIA addition:* | | | | | | |
| Plant and machinery | 280,400 | | | | | |
| AIA £500,000 × 6/12 | (250,000) | | | | | 250,000 |
| | 30,400 | 30,400 | | | | |
| *Disposal* | | (18,000) | | | | |
| | | 12,400 | | | | |
| *Non-AIA addition:* | | | | | | |
| Car | | | | 16,000 | | |
| WDA @ 18% × 6/12 | | | | (1,440) | × 75% | 1,080 |
| WDA @ 18% × 6/12 | | (1,116) | | | | 1,116 |
| Capital allowances | | | | | | 252,196 |
| **Year end 31 Dec 15** | | 11,284 | | 14,560 | | |
| *Disposal* | | | | (15,300) | | |
| Balancing charge | | | | (740) | × 75% | (555) |
| *Additions:* | | | | | | |
| Car - salesman | | | 28,000 | | | |
| Car – Mr Wish | | | | 17,500 | | |
| WDA @ 8 % | | | (2,240) | | | 2,240 |
| FYA @100% | | | | (17,500) | × 75% | 13,125 |
| WDA @ 18% | | (2,031) | | | | 2,031 |
| Capital allowances | | | | | | 16,841 |
| c/f | | 9,253 | 25,760 | 0 | | |

## Task 3

(a) **Show the division of profits between the partners for the year ended 30 September 2014 in the table below. Fill in all unshaded boxes and add a 0 (zero) if necessary.**

|  | Jude | Kelly | Liam |
|---|---|---|---|
| (xx/xx/xxxx) | £ | £ | £ |
| Period to: |  |  |  |
| 30/06/2014 |  |  |  |
| Division of profits (3:1) | 30,375 | 10,125 | 0 |
| Period to: |  |  |  |
| 30/09/2014 |  |  |  |
| Salary (3 months) | 0 | 0 | 1,500 |
| Division of profits (2:2:1) | 4,800 | 4,800 | 2,400 |
| Total profit for y/e 30/09/2014 | 35,175 | 14,925 | 3,900 |

(b)

(1) The penultimate tax year is: (insert as (xxxx/xx)

2014/15

(2) The final tax year is: (insert as (xxxx/xx)

2015/16

(3) The profits for the penultimate year of trade are:

£ 45,000

(4) The profits for the final year of trade are:

£ 47,500

(£42,000 + £15,000 – £9,500)

## Task 4

(a) **Identify how the company will deal with its capital allowances in the long period of account. Tick ONE box.**

| | ✓ |
|---|---|
| One computation from 1 January 2014 to 31 March 2015 | |
| Two computations: one from 1 January 2014 to 31 March 2014 and one from 1 April 2014 to 31 March 2015 | |
| Two computations: one from 1 January 2014 to 31 December 2014 and one from 1 January 2015 to 31 March 2015 | ✓ |
| It can deal with the computation for whatever period the company chooses | |

(b)

    (1)   Abbey Ltd's taxable total profits are:

| £ | 688,660 |
|---|---|

        (£620,843 + £67,817)

    (2)   The applicable upper limit is:

| £ | 750,000 |
|---|---|

        (£1,500,000/2)

        and the applicable lower limit is:

| £ | 150,000 |
|---|---|

        (£300,000/2)

    (3)   The corporation tax payable for the year ended 31 March 2015 is:

| £ | 144,466 |
|---|---|

        Marginal relief applies:

| | £ |
|---|---|
| £688,660 × 21% | 144,619 |
| Less 1/400 × (£750,000 – £688,660) | (153) |
| | 144,466 |

    (4)   The due date for payment is:

| 01/01/2016 |
|---|

(c) **Identify the date the company will be required to pay its FINAL instalment of the liability. Tick ONE box.**

|  | ✓ |
|---|---|
| 14 October 2014 |  |
| 14 January 2015 |  |
| 14 April 2015 | ✓ |
| 1 October 2015 |  |

## Task 5

Crystal's Class 2 NIC liability for 2014/15 is: (show your answer to the nearest penny)

| £ | 143 | • | 00 |
|---|---|---|---|

(£2.75 × 52)

Crystal's Class 4 NIC liability for 2014/15 is: (show your answer to the nearest penny)

| £ | 4,049 | • | 51 |
|---|---|---|---|

£(41,865 – 7,956) × 9% + £(91,750 – 41,865) × 2%

= (3,051.81) + (997.70)

Pearl's Class 2 NIC liability for 2014/15 is: (show your answer to the nearest penny)

| £ | 143 | • | 00 |
|---|---|---|---|

(£2.75 × 52)

Pearl's Class 4 NIC liability for 2014/15 is: (show your answer to the nearest penny)

| £ | 1,740 | • | 96 |
|---|---|---|---|

£(27,300 – 7,956) × 9%

# Task 6

(a)

|  | True ✓ | False ✓ |
|---|---|---|
| A sole trader must make a claim to set a loss made in 2014/15 against total income in 2014/15 before making a claim to set the loss against total income in 2013/14. |  | ✓ |
| A sole trader can carry trade losses forward and choose the best year to use them. |  | ✓ |
| A sole trader can only offset trading losses brought forward against profits of the same trade. | ✓ |  |

A sole trader can make a claim to deduct the loss from total income in the tax year preceding the tax year in which the loss is made whether or not he makes a claim to set it against total income in the tax year of the loss.

A sole trader must offset losses carried forward against the first available profits of the same trade.

(b)

(1) The amount of trading loss that can be claimed against profits in year ended 31 March 2015 is:

| £ | 47,150 |
|---|---|

(£52,350 - £5,200)

(2) The amount of trading loss that can be carried forward to the year ended 31 March 2016 is:

| £ | 150 |
|---|---|

## Task 7

> (a) The date by which the income tax and Class 4 NIC for 2014/15 should be paid is 31 January 2016.
>
> (b) There will be two payments on account for 2015/16. Each will be calculated as 50% of the income tax and Class 4 NIC liability for the previous tax year (2014/15). The amount will therefore be £2,112.50 (£4,225 ÷ 2), and will be payable on 31 January during the tax year (31 January 2016) and 31 July after the end of the tax year (31 July 2016).
>
> (c) A balancing payment will be due on 31 January after the end of the tax year (31 January 2017) which will calculated as the actual amount payable for 2015/16 less the two payments on account.
>
> (d) A penalty may be imposed on Mina as she has been careless and not taken reasonable care when filing her return. The penalty will be 30% of the potential lost revenue (PLR) to HMRC as a result of the error. This may be reduced to 0% if Mina makes an unprompted disclosure of the error, which would be before Mina has reason to believe HMRC might discover the error. Otherwise the penalty could be reduced to 15% of PLR and classed as a prompted disclosure.

## Task 8

| | |
|---|---|
| Box 3 | £865,000 |
| Box 5 | £865,000 |
| Box 16 | £73,500 |
| Box 18 | £73,500 |
| Box 21 | £938,500 |
| Box 37 | £938,500 |
| Box 38 | £120,000 |
| Box 39 | 1 |
| Box 43 | 2014 |
| Box 44 | £938,500 |
| Box 45 | 21% |
| Box 46 | £197,085 |
| Box 63 | £197,085 |
| Box 70 | £197,085 |

## Task 9

(a)

|  | Exempt | Chargeable |
|---|---|---|
| Disposal of a vintage car worth £40,000 | ✓ |  |
| Gift of land to a charity | ✓ |  |
| Gift of jewellery on the taxpayer's death | ✓ |  |

(b) **Calculate the chargeable gain on the disposal of the three acres of land using the table below (do not use brackets or minus signs).**

|  | £ |
|---|---|
| Gross proceeds | 105,000 |
| Costs of disposal | 1,500 |
| Net proceeds | 103,500 |
| Cost (w) | 35,000 |
| Enhancement expenditure | 2,500 |
| Chargeable gain | 66,000 |

**Working:** $\text{cost} = \dfrac{105,000}{105,000 + 45,000} \times £50,000$

(35,000)

# Task 10

| FA 1985 pool | No of shares | Cost | Indexed cost |
|---|---|---|---|
| | | £ | £ |
| April 1989 | 2,000 | 25,000 | 25,000 |
| Index to June 1994 0.266 × £25,000 | | | 6,650 |
| Addition | 2,000 | 35,000 | 35,000 |
| | 4,000 | 60,000 | 66,650 |
| Bonus issue (N) | 400 | – | – |
| | 4,400 | 60,000 | 66,650 |
| Index to September 2002 0.227 × £66,650 | | | 15,130 |
| | 4,400 | 60,000 | 81,780 |
| Rights issue | 880 | 8,800 | 8,800 |
| | 5,280 | 68,800 | 90,580 |
| Index to May 2014 0.441 × £90,580 | | | 39,946 |
| | 5,280 | 68,800 | 130,526 |
| Less sale | (4,000) | (52,121) | (98,883) |
| | 1,280 | 16,679 | 31,643 |
| Gain | | | £ |
| Disposal proceeds | | | 130,000 |
| Less cost | | | (52,121) |
| Less indexation £(98,883 – 52,121) | | | (46,762) |
| Chargeable gain | | | 31,117 |

**Note.** There is no need to compute indexation to the date of the bonus issue.

# Task 11

(a) **Identify whether the following statements are True or False.**

|  | True ✓ | False ✓ |
|---|---|---|
| If an individual has allowable capital losses brought forward, these are only used to bring gains down to the annual exempt amount. | ✓ |  |
| Allowable capital losses of the current year can be restricted to bring the net current year gains down to the annual exempt amount. |  | ✓ |
| Allowable capital losses can be carried back against gains in the previous 12 month period. |  | ✓ |

If an individual has allowable losses brought forward, these are only used to bring gains down to the annual exempt amount.

Current year losses cannot be restricted to preserve the annual exempt amount, and capital losses can never be carried back.

(b)

(1) The gain on the disposal is:

£ | 68,450

|  | £ |
|---|---|
| Sale proceeds | 260,000 |
| Less          cost | (150,000) |
| indexation allowance £150,000 × 0.277 | (41,550) |
| Chargeable gain | 68,450 |

(2) The gain immediately chargeable is:

£ | 30,000

This amount of the proceeds is not reinvested in the replacement factory.

(3) The gain rolled-over:

£ | 38,450

£(68,450 – 30,000). This remaining amount of the gain is set against the base cost of the replacement factory.

BPP
LEARNING MEDIA

# BPP PRACTICE ASSESSMENT 2
# BUSINESS TAX

**Time allowed: 2 hours**

PRACTICE ASSESSMENT 2

# Taxation Data

## Taxation tables for Business Tax – 2014/15

**Note that 'TAXATION DATA 1' and 'TAXATION DATA 2' shown below will be available as pop up windows throughout your live assessment.**

### TAXATION DATA 1

*Capital allowances*
Annual investment allowance

| | |
|---|---|
| From 1 January 2013 | £250,000 |
| From 1/6 April 2014 | £500,000 |
| Plant and machinery writing down allowance | 18% |

Motor cars

| | |
|---|---|
| $CO_2$ emissions up to 95g/km | 100% |
| $CO_2$ emissions between 96g/km and 130g/km | 18% |
| $CO_2$ emissions over 130g/km | 8% |

Energy efficient and water saving plant

| | |
|---|---|
| First year allowance | 100% |

*Capital gains*

| | |
|---|---|
| Annual exempt amount | £11,000 |
| Standard rate | 18% |
| Higher rate (applicable over £31,865) | 28% |
| Entrepreneurs' relief rate | 10% |
| Entrepreneurs' relief limit | £10,000,000 |

*National insurance rates*

| | |
|---|---|
| Class 2 contributions: | £2.75 per week |
| Small earnings exception | £5,885 p.a. |

Class 4 contributions:

| | |
|---|---|
| Main rate | 9% |
| Additional rate | 2% |
| Lower profits limit | £7,956 |
| Upper profits limit | £41,865 |

### TAXATION DATA 2

*Corporation tax*

| *Financial year* | 2014 | 2013 |
|---|---|---|
| Small profits rate | 20% | 20% |
| Marginal relief: | | |
| Lower limit | £300,000 | £300,000 |
| Upper limit | £1,500,000 | £1,500,000 |
| Standard fraction | 1/400 | 3/400 |
| Main rate | 21% | 23% |

Marginal relief formula: Fraction $\times$ (U–A) $\times$ N/A

# Business Tax BPP practice assessment 2

## Task 1

The statement of profit or loss for Henry Ltd for the year to 31 December 2014 shows the following information:

|  | £ | £ |
|---|---|---|
| Gross profit | | 487,500 |
| Profit on sale of shares | | 12,850 |
| Dividends received | | 4,500 |
| Property business income | | 7,500 |
| | | 512,350 |
| General expenses (Note 1) | 240,780 | |
| Wages and salaries | 120,650 | |
| Administrative expenses | 87,230 | |
| Depreciation charge | 14,600 | |
| | | (463,260) |
| Profit for the year | | 49,090 |

Notes include:

(1) **General expenses**

These include:

|  | £ |
|---|---|
| Qualifying charitable donation (paid July 2014) | 3,500 |
| Entertaining customers | 8,450 |

(2) **Capital allowances**

The capital allowances for the year ended 31 December 2014 are £8,750.

(a) **Complete the computation. Do not use minus signs or brackets to show negative figures. Please keep your selected answers in the same order as they appear in the picklist.**

| | | |
|---|---|---|
| Profit | | 49,090 |
| **Add back** | | |
| | ▼ | |
| | ▼ | |
| | ▼ | |
| Total added back | | |
| **Deduct** | | |
| | ▼ | |
| | ▼ | |
| | ▼ | |
| | ▼ | |
| Adjusted trading profits | | |

**Picklist 1:**

Qualifying charitable donation (paid July 2014)

Entertaining customers

Wages and salaries

Administrative expenses

Depreciation charge

**Picklist 2:**

Profit on sale of shares

Dividends received

Property business income

Administrative expenses

Depreciation charge

Capital allowances

(b) **For each of the following items, pick the correct treatment in relation to the computation of the taxable profit.**

Capital allowances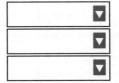

Staff party £10 per head

Purchase of new motor vehicle

**Picklist:**

Allowed
Disallowed and add back
Disallowed and deduct

## Task 2

Mustafa has been trading for many years, making up accounts to 31 December.

His capital allowances balances brought forward at 1 January 2014 were as follows:

| | |
|---|---|
| Main pool | £13,291 |
| Car for Mustafa, 30% private usage | £8,745 |

The following capital transactions were made in the period:

| Additions | | £ |
|---|---|---|
| 10.02.14 | Plant and machinery | 58,100 |
| 15.04.14 | Car for Mustafa, $CO_2$ emissions 90 g/km, 40% private usage | 24,500 |
| 22.06.14 | Plant and machinery | 365,000 |
| Disposal | | |
| 15.04.14 | Mustafa's previous car | 8,000 |
| 3.05.14 | Plant and machinery (original cost £4,100) | 5,970 |

**Using the proforma layout provided, calculate the capital allowances for the year ended 31 December 2014.**

| | AIA | Main pool | Private use car (70%) | Private use car (60%) | Allowances |
|---|---|---|---|---|---|
| | £ | £ | £ | £ | £ |
| | | | | | |
| | | | | | |
| | | | | | |
| | | | | | |
| | | | | | |
| | | | | | |
| | | | | | |
| | | | | | |
| | | | | | |
| | | | | | |
| | | | | | |
| | | | | | |
| | | | | | |
| | | | | | |

## Task 3

Sayed started trading on 1 January 2014. He makes up his accounts to 30 April each year. The profits were calculated as:

|                          | £      |
|--------------------------|--------|
| Period to 30 April 2014  | 20,000 |
| Year to 30 April 2015    | 36,000 |
| Year to 30 April 2016    | 42,000 |

**Calculate the taxable profits and state the tax year and basis period for the first three tax years of trading. Insert the tax year dates as XXXX/XX (eg 2013/14) and the basis period dates as XX/XX/XXXX (eg 01/12/2013).**

| | Tax year<br>XXXX / XX | Basis period<br>XX/XX/XXXX – XX/XX/XXXX | Profit<br>£ |
|-------------|------------|------------------------------|--------|
| First year  | ☐ / ☐ | ☐ – ☐ | ☐ |
| Second year | ☐ / ☐ | ☐ – ☐ | ☐ |
| Third year  | ☐ / ☐ | ☐ – ☐ | ☐ |

His overlap profits are:

| £ | |
|---|---|

## Task 4

A company made up accounts to 31 March 2014. It decides to make up its next set of accounts to 30 September 2015.

(a) **Show how each of the following would be allocated for the long period of account.**

|  | Amount accrued in period ✓ | Time apportioned ✓ | Period in which it arose ✓ |
|---|---|---|---|
| Trading profits |  |  |  |
| Business property income |  |  |  |
| Qualifying charitable donation |  |  |  |
| Chargeable gains |  |  |  |
| Non trading interest received |  |  |  |

(b) **Tick the correct box to show whether the following statements are True or False:**

|  | True ✓ | False ✓ |
|---|---|---|
| A company can offset its allowable losses on the disposal of chargeable assets against trading profits. |  |  |
| A company can carry back its trading losses to set against total profits of the previous 12 months before offsetting losses against current year total profits. |  |  |
| The carry forward of a company's trading loss to offset against the first available profits of the same trade is automatic and compulsory. |  |  |

A company has the following information for the year ended 31 March 2015:

- Taxable total profits are £280,000.
- Dividends received (net) are £10,800.
- The company has two associated companies.

(c) **Calculate the marginal relief that would apply.**

| Marginal relief for Finance Year 2014 | £ |
|---|---|
| 1/400 × [          ] − [          ] × [          ] / [          ] | [          ] |

## Task 5

Polly is a sole trader who has taxable trading profits of £63,000 in 2014/15.

**The amount chargeable to national insurance Class 4 contributions at 9% is:**

£ [          ]

**The amount chargeable to national insurance Class 4 contributions at 2% is:**

£ [          ]

**The total amount of national insurance payable by Polly in 2014/15 is:**

£ [          ] . [          ]

## Task 6

JDP, a sole trader who has been trading for many years, made a trading profit of £4,500 in his year ended 31 January 2014, a trading loss of £45,000 in his year ended 31 January 2015, and he predicts trading profits to be £5,000 for year ended 31 January 2016. Each tax year he also receives rental income of £9,000, and in December 2014 he sold a painting and made a chargeable gain of £17,000.

JDP has a policy of claiming the maximum amount of loss relief as early as possible, in all possible ways.

**How much trading loss will JDP relieve against net income in 2013/14?**

£ [          ]

**How much trading loss will JDP relieve against net income in 2014/15?**

£ [          ]

How much trading loss will JDP relieve against his chargeable gain in 2014/15?

£ [ ]

Tick the correct box to show whether the following statement is True or False:

|  | True ✓ | False ✓ |
|---|---|---|
| In 2014/15 JDP could choose to just set the loss against the capital gain, so as not to lose the benefit of his personal allowance | | |

What is the maximum trading loss JDP can relieve in 2015/16?

£ [ ]

........................................................................................................

## Task 7

(a) (1) **The maximum penalty for failure to keep records for each tax year or accounting period is:**

|  | ✓ |
|---|---|
| £4,000 | |
| £3,000 | |
| £2,500 | |
| £1,500 | |

(2) **The maximum penalty for a deliberate but not concealed failure to notify chargeability as a percentage of Potential Lost Revenue is:**

|  | ✓ |
|---|---|
| 70% | |
| 35% | |
| 20% | |
| 15% | |

(3) A taxpayer files his tax return for 2014/15 online on 15 March 2016. His tax liability for the year is £2,000.

**The maximum penalty for late filing is:**

|  | ✓ |
|---|---|
| £2,000 |  |
| £300 |  |
| £200 |  |
| £100 |  |

(b) Holly has a liability to capital gains tax in 2014/15.

(1) **She must pay the capital gains tax due by: (insert dates as xx/xx/xxxx)**



Holly is also required to make payments on account for her 2014/15 income tax liability.

(2) **She must make payments on account for 2014/15 by:**



**and**



(3) **She must pay the balancing payment by:**

## Task 8

Aggie Tring has carried on business for many years as a furniture restorer making up accounts to 31 December each year.

The following information is relevant to her period of account to 31 December 2014:

|  | £ |
|---|---|
| Revenue | 144,000 |
| Cost of materials used in restoration | 20,000 |
| Travel (20% private) | 5,700 |
| Electricity | 900 |
| Insurance | 360 |
| Office costs | 1,800 |
| Bank charges | 200 |
| Accountancy | 550 |
| Machinery purchased | 5,000 |

**Using this information, complete the self employment page.**

## Business expenses

Please read the *Self-employment (full) notes* before filling in this section.

| Total expenses | Disallowable expenses |
|---|---|
| If your annual turnover was below £81,000 you may just put your total expenses in box 31 | Use this column if the figures in boxes 17 to 30 include disallowable amounts |

**17** Cost of goods bought for resale or goods used

£ ⬚⬚⬚⬚⬚⬚⬚⬚ · 0 0

**32** £ ⬚⬚⬚⬚⬚⬚⬚⬚ · 0 0

**18** Construction industry - *payments to subcontractors*

£ ⬚⬚⬚⬚⬚⬚⬚⬚ · 0 0

**33** £ ⬚⬚⬚⬚⬚⬚⬚⬚ · 0 0

**19** Wages, salaries and other staff costs

£ ⬚⬚⬚⬚⬚⬚⬚⬚ · 0 0

**34** £ ⬚⬚⬚⬚⬚⬚⬚⬚ · 0 0

**20** Car, van and travel expenses

£ ⬚⬚⬚⬚⬚⬚⬚⬚ · 0 0

**35** £ ⬚⬚⬚⬚⬚⬚⬚⬚ · 0 0

**21** Rent, rates, power and insurance costs

£ ⬚⬚⬚⬚⬚⬚⬚⬚ · 0 0

**36** £ ⬚⬚⬚⬚⬚⬚⬚⬚ · 0 0

**22** Repairs and renewals of property and equipment

£ ⬚⬚⬚⬚⬚⬚⬚⬚ · 0 0

**37** £ ⬚⬚⬚⬚⬚⬚⬚⬚ · 0 0

**23** Phone, fax, stationery and other office costs

£ ⬚⬚⬚⬚⬚⬚⬚⬚ · 0 0

**38** £ ⬚⬚⬚⬚⬚⬚⬚⬚ · 0 0

**24** Advertising and business entertainment costs

£ ⬚⬚⬚⬚⬚⬚⬚⬚ · 0 0

**39** £ ⬚⬚⬚⬚⬚⬚⬚⬚ · 0 0

**25** Interest on bank and other loans

£ ⬚⬚⬚⬚⬚⬚⬚⬚ · 0 0

**40** £ ⬚⬚⬚⬚⬚⬚⬚⬚ · 0 0

**26** Bank, credit card and other financial charges

£ ⬚⬚⬚⬚⬚⬚⬚⬚ · 0 0

**41** £ ⬚⬚⬚⬚⬚⬚⬚⬚ · 0 0

**27** Irrecoverable debts written off

£ ⬚⬚⬚⬚⬚⬚⬚⬚ · 0 0

**42** £ ⬚⬚⬚⬚⬚⬚⬚⬚ · 0 0

**28** Accountancy, legal and other professional fees

£ ⬚⬚⬚⬚⬚⬚⬚⬚ · 0 0

**43** £ ⬚⬚⬚⬚⬚⬚⬚⬚ · 0 0

**29** Depreciation and loss/profit on sale of assets

£ ⬚⬚⬚⬚⬚⬚⬚⬚ · 0 0

**44** £ ⬚⬚⬚⬚⬚⬚⬚⬚ · 0 0

**30** Other business expenses

£ ⬚⬚⬚⬚⬚⬚⬚⬚ · 0 0

**45** £ ⬚⬚⬚⬚⬚⬚⬚⬚ · 0 0

**31** Total expenses (total of boxes 17 to 30)

£ ⬚⬚⬚⬚⬚⬚⬚⬚ · 0 0

**46** Total disallowable expenses (total of boxes 32 to 45)

£ ⬚⬚⬚⬚⬚⬚⬚⬚ · 0 0

SA103F 2014                    Page SEF 2

## Task 9

(a) Old Ltd bought a plot of land in November 2010 for £70,000. It paid legal fees of £1,500 on the acquisition. Old Ltd sold the land for £125,000 in March 2015. It spent £500 advertising the land and £1,800 on legal fees.

**Assumed Indexation factor**

November 2010 to March 2015     0.157

**Net proceeds are:**

£ [          ]

**The allowable cost is:**

£ [          ]

**Indexation allowance is:**

£ [          ]

**The chargeable gain on the sale is:**

£ [          ]

(b) **For the following disposals, tick whether they would be exempt or chargeable.**

|  | Exempt | Chargeable |
|---|---|---|
| Gift of antique jewellery from husband to wife | ☐ | ☐ |
| Gift of car from mother to son | ☐ | ☐ |
| Gift of property from mother to son on her death | ☐ | ☐ |

## Task 10

Purple Ltd had the following transactions in the shares of Yellow Ltd:

| May 1989 | Purchased 4,000 shares for £8,000 |
| May 2003 | Took up one for two rights issue at £3 per share |
| October 2014 | Sold all the shares for £32,000 |

**Assumed Indexation factors**

| May 1989 to May 2003 | 0.578 |
| May 2003 to October 2014 | 0.425 |

**Using the proforma layout provided, calculate the chargeable gain arising from the sale of the shares in Yellow Ltd.**

*Share pool*

|  | No of shares | Cost | Indexed cost |
|---|---|---|---|
|  |  | £ | £ |
|  |  |  |  |
|  |  |  |  |
|  |  |  |  |
|  |  |  |  |
|  |  |  |  |
|  |  |  |  |
|  |  |  |  |
|  |  |  |  |

*Gain*

|  | £ |
|---|---|
|  |  |
|  |  |
|  |  |
|  |  |
|  |  |

## Task 11

Georgia sold her business which she had run for twenty years to Milly on 10 October 2014. The only chargeable asset was her shop which Georgia had bought in February 2007 for £82,500. She spent £17,000 on building an extension in June 2009. The sale proceeds relating to the shop were £225,000. Georgia claimed entrepreneurs' relief on the disposal.

(a) **Using the proforma layout provided, calculate Georgia's capital gains tax liability for 2014/15. She had made no other chargeable gains during the year.**

|  | £ |
|---|---|
| Sale proceeds |  |
| cost |  |
| enhancement expenditure |  |
| Net gain |  |
| annual exempt amount |  |
| Taxable gain |  |
| CGT payable |  |

On 1 November 2014 Mike sold a factory used in his business for £600,000. The factory had cost £175,000. Mike had purchased a replacement factory for £750,000 on 1 September 2014.

(b) **How much of Mike's capital gain on the disposal of the original factory can be deferred by a rollover relief claim?**

|  | ✓ |
|---|---|
| £150,000 |  |
| £575,000 |  |
| £175,000 |  |
| £425,000 |  |

(c) If Mike's replacement factory had instead cost him £500,000, **the amount of the gain that would be chargeable to CGT in 2014/15 is:**

£ _____

# BPP PRACTICE ASSESSMENT 2
# BUSINESS TAX


# ANSWERS

# Business Tax BPP practice assessment 2

## Task 1

(a) Complete the computation. Do not use minus signs or brackets to show negative figures. Please keep your selected answers in the same order as they appear in the picklist.

| Profit | | 49,090 |
|---|---|---|
| **Add back** | | |
| Qualifying charitable donation (paid July 2014) | ▼ | 3,500 |
| Entertaining customers | ▼ | 8,450 |
| Depreciation charge | ▼ | 14,600 |
| Total added back | | 26,550 |
| **Deduct** | | |
| Profit on sale of shares | ▼ | 12,850 |
| Dividends received | ▼ | 4,500 |
| Property business income | ▼ | 7,500 |
| Capital allowances | ▼ | 8,750 |
| Adjusted trading profits | | 42,040 |

(b) For each of the following items, pick the correct treatment in relation to the computation of the taxable profit.

| | |
|---|---|
| Capital allowances | Allowed ▼ |
| Staff party £10 per head | Allowed ▼ |
| Purchase of new motor vehicle | Disallowed and add back ▼ |

## Task 2

*Year ended 31 December 2014*

| | AIA | Main pool | Private use car (70%) | Private use car (60%) | Allowances |
|---|---|---|---|---|---|
| | £ | £ | £ | £ | £ |
| b/f | | 13,291 | 8,745 | | |
| *AIA additions* | | | | | |
| February 2014 | 58,100 | | | | |
| June 2014 | 365,000 | | | | |
| AIA (note) | (423,100) | | | | 423,100 |
| | 0 | | | | |
| *Non-AIA* | | | | | |
| Car April 2014 | | | | 24,500 | |
| Disposals | | (4,100) | (8,000) | | |
| | | 9,191 | | | |
| BA | | | 745 × 70% | | 522 |
| WDA @ 18% | | (1,654) | | | 1,654 |
| FYA @ 100% | | | | (24,500) × 60% | 14,700 |
| c/f | | 7,537 | | 0 | |
| Total allowances | | | | | 439,976 |

**Note:** Max AIA for year ended 31 December 2014 = £437,500 (£250,000 × 3/12 + £500,000 × 9/12)

## Task 3

Calculate the taxable profits and state the tax year and basis period for the first three tax years of trading. Insert the tax year dates as XXXX/XX (eg 2013/14) and the basis period dates as XX/XX/XXXX (eg 01/12/2013).

| | Tax year<br>YYYY / YY | Basis period<br>XX/XX/XXXX – XX/XX/XXXX | Profit<br>£ |
|---|---|---|---|
| First year | 2013 / 14 | 01/01/2014 – 05/04/2014 | 15,000 |
| Second year | 2014 / 15 | 01/01/2014 – 31/12/2014 | 44,000 |
| Third year | 2015 / 16 | 01/05/2014 – 30/04/2015 | 36,000 |

His overlap profits are:

| £ | 39,000 |
|---|---|

Overlap period: 1 January 2014 to 5 April 2014 and 1 May 2014 to 31 December 2014

Overlap profits: ¾ × £20,000 + 8/12 × £36,000

## Task 4

(a) Show how each of the following would be allocated for the long period of account.

| | Amount accrued in period<br>✓ | Time apportioned<br>✓ | Period in which it arose<br>✓ |
|---|---|---|---|
| Trading profits | | ✓ | |
| Business property income | | ✓ | |
| Qualifying charitable donation | | | ✓ |
| Chargeable gains | | | ✓ |
| Non trading interest received | ✓ | | |

(b) Tick the correct box to show whether the following statements are True or False:

| | True ✓ | False ✓ |
|---|---|---|
| A company can offset its allowable losses on the disposal of chargeable assets against trading profits. | | ✓ |
| A company can carry back its trading losses to set against total profits of the previous 12 months before offsetting losses against current year total profits. | | ✓ |
| The carry forward of a company's trading loss to offset against the first available profits of the same trade is automatic and compulsory. | ✓ | |

A company can offset its allowable losses on the disposal of chargeable assets only against chargeable gains.

A company must offset trading losses in the current period first, whereas an individual trader can offset trading losses in the current and prior year in any order.

(c) Calculate the marginal relief that would apply.

| Marginal relief for Finance Year 2014 | £ |
|---|---|
| 1/400 × [ 500,000 ] − [ 292,000 ] × $\dfrac{280,000}{292,000}$ | 499 |

··············································································

## Task 5

The amount chargeable to national insurance Class 4 contributions at 9% is:

| £ | 33,909 |
|---|---|

£(41,865 − 7,956)

The amount chargeable to national insurance Class 4 contributions at 2% is:

| £ | 21,135 |
|---|---|

£(63,000 − 41,865)

The total amount of national insurance payable by Polly for 2014/15 is:

| £ | 3,617 | . | 51 |
|---|---|---|---|

Class 2 = £2.75 × 52 weeks = £143.00

Class 4 = £33,909 × 9% + £21,135 × 2% = £3,474.51

··············································································

## Task 6

How much trading loss will JDP relieve against net income in 2013/14?

| £ | 13,500 |
|---|--------|

(£4,500 + £9,000) The loss cannot be restricted to save the personal allowance

How much trading loss will JDP relieve against net income in 2014/15?

| £ | 9,000 |
|---|-------|

The loss cannot be restricted to save the personal allowance

How much trading loss will JDP relieve against his chargeable gain in 2014/15?

| £ | 17,000 |
|---|--------|

The loss cannot be restricted to save the annual exempt amount (only capital losses brought forward can be restricted in this way).

Tick the correct box to show whether the following statements are True or False:

|  | True ✓ | False ✓ |
|--|--------|---------|
| In 2014/15 JDP could choose to just set the loss against the capital gain, so as not to lose the benefit of his personal allowance |  | ✓ |

In order to use the trading loss against the gain, JDP must offset the loss against net income first, despite the fact that it would have been covered by his personal allowance.

What is the maximum trading loss JDP can relieve in 2015/16?

| £ | 5,000 |
|---|-------|

Losses can only be offset against trading profits when carried forward.

........................................................................................

## Task 7

(a) (1) The maximum penalty for failure to keep records for each tax year or accounting period is:

|  | ✓ |
|--------|---|
| £4,000 |  |
| £3,000 | ✓ |
| £2,500 |  |
| £1,500 |  |

(2)  The maximum penalty for a deliberate but not concealed failure to notify chargeability as a percentage of Potential Lost Revenue is:

|  | ✓ |
| --- | --- |
| 70% | ✓ |
| 35% | |
| 20% | |
| 15% | |

(3)  A taxpayer files his tax return for 2014/15 online on 15 March 2016. His tax liability for the year is £2,000.

The maximum penalty for late filing is:

|  | ✓ |
| --- | --- |
| £2,000 | |
| £300 | |
| £200 | |
| £100 | ✓ |

Initial penalty for filing return late is £100. As it is less than 3 months late no further penalty is payable.

(b)  (1)  She must pay the capital gains tax due by: (insert dates as xx/xx/xxxx)

31/01/2016

(2)  She must make payments on account for 2014/15 by:

31/01/2015

and

31/07/2015

(3)  She must pay the balancing payment by:

31/01/2016

## Task 8

| Box 17 | £20000.00 |
|--------|-----------|
| Box 20 | £5700.00 |
| Box 21 | £1260.00 |
| Box 23 | £1800.00 |
| Box 26 | £200.00 |
| Box 28 | £550.00 |
| Box 31 | £29510.00 |
| Box 35 | £1140.00 |
| Box 46 | £1140.00 |

## Task 9

(a)

Net proceeds are:

| £ | 122,700 |
|---|---------|

(£125,000 – £500 – £1,800)

The allowable cost is:

| £ | 71,500 |
|---|--------|

Indexation allowance is:

| £ | 11,226 |
|---|--------|

(0.157 × £71,500)

The chargeable gain on the sale is:

| £ | 39,974 |
|---|--------|

(b)     For the following disposals, tick whether they would be exempt or chargeable.

|  | Exempt | Chargeable |
|---|---|---|
| Gift of antique jewellery from husband to wife |  | ✓ |
| Gift of car from mother to son | ✓ |  |
| Gift of property from mother to son on her death | ✓ |  |

Note the gift between husband and wife is not exempt; it is transferred at no gain, no loss, with deemed proceeds equal to the original cost.

Cars are exempt assets and transfers on death are always exempt from capital gains tax.

## Task 10

*Share pool*

|  | No of shares | Cost £ | Indexed cost £ |
|---|---|---|---|
| May 1989 | 4,000 | 8,000 | 8,000 |
| Indexed rise to May 2003 |  |  |  |
| £8,000 × 0.578 |  |  | 4,624 |
|  |  |  | 12,624 |
| Rights issue 1:2 @ £3 | 2,000 | 6,000 | 6,000 |
|  | 6,000 | 14,000 | 18,624 |
| Indexed rise to October 2014 |  |  |  |
| £18,624 × 0.425 |  |  | 7,915 |
|  | 6,000 | 14,000 | 26,539 |

*Gain*

|  | £ |
|---|---|
| Disposal proceeds | 32,000 |
| Less cost | (14,000) |
|  | 18,000 |
| Less indexation (£26,539 – £14,000) | (12,539) |
| Chargeable gain | 5,461 |

# Task 11

(a) Using the proforma layout provided, calculate Georgia's capital gains tax liability for 2014/15. She had made no other chargeable gains during the year.

|  | £ |
|---|---|
| Sale proceeds | 225,000 |
| cost | (82,500) |
| enhancement expenditure | (17,000) |
| Net gain | 125,500 |
| annual exempt amount | (11,000) |
| Taxable gain | 114,500 |
| CGT payable @ 10% | 11,450 |

(b) How much of Mike's capital gain on the disposal of the original factory can be deferred by a rollover relief claim?

|  | ✓ |
|---|---|
| £150,000 |  |
| £575,000 |  |
| £175,000 |  |
| £425,000 | ✓ |

|  | £ |
|---|---|
| Proceeds | 600,000 |
| Less cost | (175,000) |
| Chargeable gain | 425,000 |

Mike reinvested all of the proceeds in a replacement business asset in the period 12 months before/3 years after the disposal so the whole gain of £425,000 can be rolled-over.

(c) The amount of the gain that would be chargeable to CGT in 2014/15 is:

| £ | 100,000 |
|---|---|

This is the amount of proceeds that have not been reinvested.

# BPP PRACTICE ASSESSMENT 3
# BUSINESS TAX

Time allowed: 2 hours

BPP PRACTICE ASSESSMENT 3
BUSINESS TAX

Time allowed: 2 hours

# Taxation Data

## Taxation tables for Business Tax – 2014/15

**Note that 'TAXATION DATA 1' and 'TAXATION DATA 2' shown below will be available as pop up windows throughout your live assessment.**

## TAXATION DATA 1

*Capital allowances*

Annual investment allowance

| | |
|---|---|
| From 1 January 2013 | £250,000 |
| From 1/6 April 2014 | £500,000 |
| Plant and machinery writing down allowance | 18% |

Motor cars

| | |
|---|---|
| $CO_2$ emissions up to 95g/km | 100% |
| $CO_2$ emissions between 96g/km and 130g/km | 18% |
| $CO_2$ emissions over 130g/km | 8% |

Energy efficient and water saving plant

| | |
|---|---|
| First year allowance | 100% |

*Capital gains*

| | |
|---|---|
| Annual exempt amount | £11,000 |
| Standard rate | 18% |
| Higher rate (applicable over £31,865) | 28% |
| Entrepreneurs' relief rate | 10% |
| Entrepreneurs' relief limit | £10,000,000 |

*National insurance rates*

| | |
|---|---|
| Class 2 contributions: | £2.75 per week |
| Small earnings exception | £5,885 p.a. |

Class 4 contributions:

| | |
|---|---|
| Main rate | 9% |
| Additional rate | 2% |
| Lower profits limit | £7,956 |
| Upper profits limit | £41,865 |

## TAXATION DATA 2

*Corporation tax*

| Financial year | 2014 | 2013 |
|---|---|---|
| Small profits rate | 20% | 20% |
| Marginal relief: | | |
| Lower limit | £300,000 | £300,000 |
| Upper limit | £1,500,000 | £1,500,000 |
| Standard fraction | 1/400 | 3/400 |
| Main rate | 21% | 23% |

Marginal relief formula: Fraction $\times$ (U–A) $\times$ N/A

# Business Tax BPP practice assessment 3

## Task 1

You have been given the following information about Robbie Ltd that relates to the year ended 31 March 2015:

| | £ | £ |
|---|---:|---:|
| Gross profit | | 801,220 |
| Profit on sale of shares | | 45,777 |
| Dividends received | | 40,500 |
| | | 887,497 |
| General expenses (Note 1) | 455,100 | |
| Administrative expenses | 122,010 | |
| Wages and salaries | 137,567 | (714,677) |
| Profit for the year | | 172,820 |

**Note 1:** General expenses:

| These include: | £ |
|---|---:|
| Qualifying charitable donation | 5,000 |
| Parking fines paid for a director | 160 |
| Depreciation charge | 65,230 |
| Subscription to a trade association | 1,000 |
| Donation to a political party | 850 |

**Note 2:** Capital allowances:

These have already been calculated at £38,750.

(a) **Complete the computation. Do not use minus signs or brackets to show negative figures. Please keep your selected answers in the same order as they appear in the picklist.**

| Profit | 172,820 |
|---|---:|
| Disallowed items added back | |
| ▼ | |
| ▼ | |
| ▼ | |

| | ▼ | |
|---|---|---|
| Total added back | | |
| **Allowed items deducted** | | |
| | ▼ | |
| | ▼ | |
| | ▼ | |
| Total deducted | | |
| Adjusted trading profits | | |

**Picklist 1:**

Qualifying charitable donation

Parking fines paid for a director

Depreciation charge

Subscription to a trade association

Donation to a political party

Administrative expenses

Wages and salaries

**Picklist 2:**

Profit on sale of shares

Dividends received

Administrative expenses

Wages and salaries

Capital allowances

(b) **Identify whether the following statements are True or False.**

| | True | False |
|---|---|---|
| Badges of trade have developed mainly through case law. | ☐ | ☐ |
| If a trader inherits an asset and he sells it shortly afterwards, it will appear likely that he is trading. | ☐ | ☐ |
| If a trader enhances an asset to make it more desirable to a buyer, this is indicative of trading. | ☐ | ☐ |

## Task 2

Ian Goodwin commenced trading on 1 May 2014, and made his first accounts up to 31 July 2015. Ian Goodwin's capital transactions from the date of commencement are:

| Additions: | | £ |
|---|---|---|
| 1 May 2014 | Plant and machinery | 400,000 |
| 1 May 2014 | Motor van | 35,000 |
| 1 October 2014 | Plant and machinery | 223,750 |
| 1 November 2014 | Car, 30% private usage by Ian ($CO_2$ emissions 172g/km) | 9,600 |
| 15 July 2015 | Car, 20% private usage by an employee ($CO_2$ emissions 92g/km) | 12,500 |

**Calculate the capital allowances for the 15-month period ended 31 July 2015.**

| | | | | | |
|---|---|---|---|---|---|
| | | | | | |
| | | | | | |
| | | | | | |
| | | | | | |
| | | | | | |
| | | | | | |
| | | | | | |
| | | | | | |
| | | | | | |
| | | | | | |
| | | | | | |
| | | | | | |
| | | | | | |
| | | | | | |
| | | | | | |

## Task 3

Gerry and Harold have been in partnership for many years making up accounts to 31 December each year sharing profits 2:1 respectively.

On 1 January 2015, Iris joined the partnership. Profits are then shared 2:2:1 for Gerry, Harold and Iris.

For the year ended 31 December 2014, the partnership trading profit was £27,000 and for the year ended 31 December 2015 was £35,000.

(1) **Using the proforma layout provided, show the division of profit between the partners for the year ended 31 December 2014 and 31 December 2015. Fill in all boxes and add a 0 (zero) if necessary.**

|  | Total £ | Gerry £ | Harold £ | Iris £ |
|---|---|---|---|---|
| Year ended 31.12.14 |  |  |  |  |
| Year ended 31.12.15 |  |  |  |  |

(2) **The taxable trading profit for each partner for 2014/15 is:**

Gerry:

£ [        ]

Harold:

£ [        ]

Iris:

£ [        ]

## Task 4

Z plc makes up accounts for a 15 month period to 31 March 2015.

(a) **Identify how the company will apportion its property income for the long period of account between the accounting periods. Tick ONE box.**

|  | ✓ |
|---|---|
| Any way the company chooses |  |
| On a time basis |  |
| On an accruals basis |  |
| On a receipts basis |  |

(b)  **Decide how the company will deal with its capital allowances computations for the long period of account. Tick ONE box.**

|  | ✓ |
|---|---|
| One computation for the whole 15 month period prorating the allowances up accordingly | |
| Two computations; one for 12 months, and one for 3 months prorating the allowances down accordingly | |

A company has the following information for the year ended 31 March 2015:

- Taxable total profits are £850,000.
- Dividends received (net) are £135,000.
- The company has no associated companies.

(c)  **Calculate the marginal relief that would apply.**

| Marginal relief for Finance Year 2014 | £ |
|---|---|
| 1/400 × [        ] – [        ] × $\dfrac{[\quad]}{[\quad]}$ | [        ] |

## Task 5

Jayden starts in business as a sole trader on 6 April 2014. Her annual accounting profit for 2014/15 is £5,700 and her adjusted trading profit for the year to 5 April 2015 is £8,100.

(1)  **Jayden's Class 2 NICs payable for 2014/15 are:**

£ [        ] . [        ]

(2)  **Jayden's Class 4 NICs payable for 2014/15 are:**

£ [        ] . [        ]

## Task 6

Zowie made a trading loss of £10,000 in her period of account to 31 March 2015.

**Identify whether the following statements are True or False.**

|  | True ✓ | False ✓ |
|---|---|---|
| Zowie can set the loss against her general income in 2014/15. |  |  |
| Zowie can carry the loss forward against her trading profits in 2015/16. |  |  |
| Zowie can set the loss against her general income in 2015/16. |  |  |
| Zowie can set the loss against her general income in 2013/14. |  |  |

## Task 7

You have been instructed by a new client who started trading on 1 May 2014. He is concerned about some important dates when he should contact HM Revenue & Customs. He has never filled in a tax return.

State:

(1) **The date when he should inform HM Revenue & Customs that he is liable to Class 2 contributions. (insert dates as xx/xx/xxxx)**

(2) **The date when he should inform HM Revenue & Customs that he is chargeable to income tax.**

(3) **The date when his first tax return should be filed, if it is to be filed online.**

## Task 8

You act for Freshly Fish, a partnership of fishmongers. The partners are Fred Fisher and his son George. The partnership profits are divided 2:1 between Fred and George. The partnership makes up accounts to 31 March each year.

The following information relates to the year to 31 March 2015:

|  | £ |
|---|---|
| Revenue | 210,000 |
| Cost of fish sold | 70,000 |
| Allowable expenses | 69,710 |
| Capital allowances | 13,200 |

**Use this information to complete page 6 of the partnership tax return for Fred Fisher.**

## PARTNERSHIP STATEMENT (SHORT) *for the year ended 5 April 2015*

*Please read these instructions before completing the Statement*

Use these pages to allocate partnership income if the only income for the relevant return period was trading and professional income or taxed interest and alternative finance receipts from banks and building societies. Otherwise you must download or ask the SA Orderline for the *Partnership Statement (Full)* pages to record details of the allocation of all the partnership income. Go to hmrc.gov.uk/selfassessmentforms

Step 1  Fill in boxes 1 to 29 and boxes A and B as appropriate. Get the figures you need from the relevant boxes in the Partnership Tax Return. Complete a separate Statement for each accounting period covered by this Partnership Tax Return and for each trade or profession carried on by the partnership.

Step 2  Then allocate the amounts in boxes 11 to 29 attributable to each partner using the allocation columns on this page and page 7, read the Partnership Tax Return Guide, go to hmrc.gov.uk/selfassessmentforms If the partnership has more than three partners, please photocopy page 7.

Step 3  Each partner will need a copy of their allocation of income to fill in their personal tax return.

### PARTNERSHIP INFORMATION
If the partnership business includes a trade or profession, enter here the accounting period for which appropriate items in this statement are returned.

Start **1** [ / / ]

End **2** [ / / ]

Nature of trade **3** [                    ]

### MIXED PARTNERSHIPS

Tick here if this Statement is drawn up using Corporation Tax rules **4** [ ]

Tick here if this Statement is drawn up using tax rules for non-residents **5** [ ]

### Individual partner details

**6** Name of partner

Address

Postcode

Date appointed as a partner
(if during 2013–14 or 2014–15)

**7** [ / / ]

Date ceased to be a partner
(if during 2013–14 or 2014–15)

**9** [ / / ]

Partner's Unique Taxpayer Reference (UTR)

**8** [          ]

Partner's National Insurance number

**10** [          ]

### Partnership's profits, losses, income, tax credits, etc.

Tick this box if the items entered in the box had foreign tax taken off

### Partner's share of profits, losses, income, tax credits, etc.

Copy figures in boxes 11 to 29 to boxes in the individual's **Partnership (short)** pages as shown below

* **for an accounting period ended in 2014–15** ▼

| | | | | |
|---|---|---|---|---|
| from box 3.83 Profit from a trade or profession | **A** | **11** £ | Profit **11** £ | Copy this figure to box 8 |
| from box 3.82 Adjustment on change of basis | | **11A** £ | **11A** £ | Copy this figure to box 10 |
| from box 3.84 Loss from a trade or profession | **B** | **12** £ | Loss **12** £ | Copy this figure to box 8 |
| from box 10.4 Business Premises Renovation Allowance | | **12A** £ | **12A** £ | Copy this figure to box 15 |

* **for the period 6 April 2014 to 5 April 2015\***

| | | | |
|---|---|---|---|
| from box 7.9A UK taxed interest and taxed alternative finance receipts | **22** £ | **22** £ | Copy this figure to box 28 |
| from box 3.97 CIS deductions made by contractors on account of tax | **24** £ | **24** £ | Copy this figure to box 30 |
| from box 3.98 Other tax taken off trading income | **24A** £ | **24A** £ | Copy this figure to box 31 |
| from box 7.8A Income Tax taken off | **25** £ | **25** £ | Copy this figure to box 29 |
| from box 3.117 Partnership charges | **29** £ | **29** £ | Copy this figure to box 4, 'Other tax reliefs' section on page Ai 2 in your personal tax return |

\* if you are a 'CT Partnership' see the Partnership Tax Return Guide

SA800 2015          PARTNERSHIP TAX RETURN: PAGE 6

## Task 9

Jakub bought a holiday cottage for £64,000 incurring legal costs of £1,200 on the purchase. He spent £12,000 on adding an extension to the cottage but had to remove it as he had not obtained planning permission.

Jakub sold the cottage for £90,000 in September 2014. He paid estate agent's fees of £1,800 and legal costs of £700.

(a) **Complete the following computation. Fill in all boxes. Add a 0 (zero) if necessary.**

£

Proceeds

Disposal costs

Costs of acquisition

Enhancement expenditure

Chargeable gain

(b) **For the following assets, tick if a disposal would be exempt or chargeable.**

|  | Exempt | Chargeable |
|---|---|---|
| Porsche car worth £120,000 | ☐ | ☐ |
| Necklace sold for £5,000, cost £2,000 | ☐ | ☐ |
| Shares in unlisted company worth £12,000 | ☐ | ☐ |

## Task 10

Treasure Ltd sold 2,500 shares in Williams Ltd for £102,100 in June 2014.

2,000 shares had been bought in November 2001 for £50,000.

In February 2000, Treasure Ltd took up a rights issue of 1 for 2 shares, at £20 per share.

**Indexation factors**

November 2001 to February 2006          0.119

February 2006 to June 2014              0.320

**Using the proforma layout provided, calculate the capital gain arising from the disposal of the shares in Williams Ltd. Clearly show the number of shares, and their value, to carry forward.**

*Share pool*

| | No. of shares | Cost £ | Indexed cost £ |
|---|---|---|---|
| | | | |
| | | | |
| | | | |
| | | | |
| | | | |
| | | | |
| | | | |
| | | | |
| | | | |
| | | | |
| | | | |
| | | | |
| | | | |
| | | | |
| | | | |
| | | | |
| | | | |
| | | | |
| | | | |

*Gain*

| | £ |
|---|---|
| | |
| | |
| | |
| | |
| | |

## Task 11

(a) DEF plc bought a factory for use in its trade on 10 December 2008 for £120,000. It sold the factory for £230,000 on 1 May 2014.

**Assumed Indexation factors**

December 2008 to May 2014       0.202

(1) **The gain on disposal of the factory is:**

£ [        ]

(2) **The dates during which a new asset must be acquired for a rollover relief claim to be made are between: (insert dates as xx/xx/xxxx)**

[        ]

**and**

[        ]

(3) **If a new factory is acquired for £200,000, the amount of the gain which can be rolled-over is:**

£ [        ]

Sami gives a shop which he has used in his trade to his son Troy in August 2014. The shop was acquired for £120,000 and was worth £150,000 at the date of the gift. A claim for gift relief is made.

(b) **Identify which of the following statements are correct.**

| | ✓ |
|---|---|
| Troy will acquire the shop at a cost of £120,000. | |
| Sami will have no chargeable gain on the gift. | |
| The annual exempt amount is deducted before gift relief. | |
| Troy will acquire the shop at a cost of £150,000. | |

# BPP PRACTICE ASSESSMENT 3
# BUSINESS TAX


# ANSWERS

# Business Tax BPP practice assessment 3

## Task 1

(a) Complete the computation. Do not use minus signs or brackets to show negative figures. Please keep your selected answers in the same order as they appear in the picklist.

| Profit | | 172,820 |
|---|---|---|
| **Disallowed items added back** | | |
| Qualifying charitable donation | ▼ | 5,000 |
| Parking fines paid for a director | ▼ | 160 |
| Depreciation charge | ▼ | 65,230 |
| Donation to a political party | ▼ | 850 |
| Total added back | | 71,240 |
| **Allowed items deducted** | | |
| Profit on sale of shares | ▼ | 45,777 |
| Dividends received | ▼ | 40,500 |
| Capital allowances | ▼ | 38,750 |
| Total deducted | | 125,027 |
| Adjusted trading profits | | 119,033 |

(b) Identify whether the following statements are True or False.

| | True | False |
|---|---|---|
| Badges of trade have developed mainly through case law. | ✓ | |
| If a trader inherits an asset and he sells it shortly afterwards, it will appear likely that he is trading. | | ✓ |
| If a trader enhances an asset to make it more desirable to a buyer, this is indicative of trading. | ✓ | |

## Task 2

|  | AIA | FYA | Main pool | Car (70%) | Allowances |
|---|---|---|---|---|---|
|  | £ | £ | £ | £ | £ |
| *AIA additions* |  |  |  |  |  |
| Plant and machinery | 400,000 |  |  |  |  |
| Motor van | 35,000 |  |  |  |  |
| Plant and machinery | 223,750 |  |  |  |  |
|  | 658,750 |  |  |  |  |
| AIA £500,000 × 15/12 (max) | (625,000) |  |  |  | 625,000 |
|  | 33,750 |  |  |  |  |
| Transfer balance to main pool | (33,750) |  | 33,750 |  |  |
| *Non-AIA addition* |  |  |  |  |  |
| Car |  |  |  | 9,600 |  |
| Car |  | 12,500 |  |  |  |
| FYA @ 100% |  | (12,500) |  |  | 12,500 |
| WDA @ 18% × 15/12 |  |  | (7,594) |  | 7,594 |
| WDA @ 8% × 15/12 |  |  |  | (960) × 70% | 672 |
|  |  |  |  |  |  |
| c/f |  |  | 26,156 | 8,640 |  |
| Allowances |  |  |  |  | 645,766 |

**Note**. Both the AIA and the WDA are time apportioned for a long period of account, but not the FYA.

## Task 3

(1)

|  | Total £ | Gerry £ | Harold £ | Iris £ |
|---|---|---|---|---|
| Year ended 31.12.14 | 27,000 | 18,000 | 9,000 | 0 |
| Year ended 31.12.15 | 35,000 | 14,000 | 14,000 | 7,000 |

(2) The taxable trading profit for each partner for 2014/15 is:

Gerry £ 18,000

Harold £ 9,000

Iris £ 1,750

*Gerry and Harold*

y/e 31.12.14 current year basis

*Iris*

First year of trading: actual basis 1 January 2015 to 5 April 2015

3/12 × £7,000

····················································································

## Task 4

(a) Identify how the company will apportion its property income for the long period of account between the accounting periods. Tick ONE box.

|  | ✓ |
|---|---|
| Any way the company chooses |  |
| On a time basis | ✓ |
| On an accruals basis |  |
| On a receipts basis |  |

(b) Decide how the company will deal with its capital allowances computations for the long period of account. Tick ONE box.

| | ✓ |
|---|---|
| One computation for the whole 15 month period prorating the allowances up accordingly | |
| Two computations; one for 12 months, and one for 3 months prorating the allowances down accordingly | ✓ |

A company has the following information for the year ended 31 March 2015:

- Taxable total profits are £850,000.
- Dividends received (net) are £135,000.
- The company has no associated companies.

(c) **Calculate the marginal relief that would apply.**

| Marginal relief for Finance Year 2014 | £ |
|---|---|
| 1/400 × [ 1,500,000 ] − [ 1,000,000 ] × $\dfrac{850,000}{1,000,000}$ | 1,063 |

.................................................................................................................

# Task 5

(1) Jayden's Class 2 NICs payable for 2014/15 are:

| £ | 0 | • | 00 |
|---|---|---|---|

Jayden's accounting profit for 2014/15 is less than £5,885 so the small earnings exception applies.

(2) Jayden's Class 4 NICs payable for 2014/15 are:

| £ | 12 | • | 96 |
|---|---|---|---|

£(8,100 − 7,956) = £144 × 9%

.................................................................................................................

## Task 6

**Identify whether the following statements are True or False.**

|  | True ✓ | False ✓ |
|---|---|---|
| Zowie can set the loss against her general income in 2014/15. | ✓ | |
| Zowie can carry the loss forward against her trading profits in 2015/16. | ✓ | |
| Zowie can set the loss against her general income in 2015/16. | | ✓ |
| Zowie can set the loss against her general income in 2013/14. | ✓ | |

## Task 7

(1) The date when he should inform HM Revenue & Customs that he is liable to Class 2 contributions.

> 31/01/2016

(2) The date when he should inform HM Revenue & Customs that he is chargeable to income tax.

> 05/10/2015

(3) The date when his first tax return should be filed, if it is to be filed online.

> 31/01/2016

## Task 8

Partnership tax adjusted trading profit £(210,000 – 70,000 – 69,710 – 13,200) = £57,090

Page 6

| Box 1 | 01.04.14 |
|---|---|
| Box 2 | 31.03.15 |
| Box 3 | Fishmongers |
| Box 11 | 57090.00 |
| Box 6 | Fred Fisher |
| Box 11 | 38060.00 |

# Task 9

(a)

|  | £ |
|---|---|
| Proceeds | 90,000 |
| Disposal costs £(1,800 + 700) | (2,500) |
| Costs of acquisition £(64,000 + 1,200) | (65,200) |
| Enhancement expenditure (not reflected in value on disposal) | 0 |
| Chargeable gain | 22,300 |

(b)

|  | Exempt | Chargeable |
|---|---|---|
| Porsche car worth £120,000 | ✓ |  |
| Necklace sold for £5,000, cost £2,000 | ✓ |  |
| Shares in unlisted company worth £12,000 |  | ✓ |

## Task 10

*Share pool*

| | No of Shares | Cost | Indexed cost |
|---|---|---|---|
| | | £ | £ |
| November 2001 | 2,000 | 50,000 | 50,000 |
| Index to February 2006 | | | |
| £50,000 × 0.119 | | | 5,950 |
| Rights issue 1 for 2 @ £20 each | 1,000 | 20,000 | 20,000 |
| | 3,000 | 70,000 | 75,950 |
| Index to June 2014 | | | |
| £75,950 × 0.320 | | | 24,304 |
| | 3,000 | 70,000 | 100,254 |
| Less sale | (2,500) | (58,333) | (83,545) |
| Carry forward | 500 | 11,667 | 16,709 |
| | | | |
| *Gain* | | | £ |
| Disposal proceeds | | | 102,100 |
| Less cost | | | (58,333) |
| | | | 43,767 |
| Indexation (83,545 – 58,333) | | | (25,212) |
| Chargeable gain | | | 18,555 |

## Task 11

(a)  (1)  The gain on disposal of the factory is:

£ | 85,760

|  | £ |
|---|---|
| Proceeds of sale | 230,000 |
| Less cost | (120,000) |
|  | 110,000 |
| Less indexation allowance £120,000 × 0.202 | (24,240) |
| Chargeable gain | 85,760 |

(2)  The dates during which a new asset must be acquired for a rollover relief claim to be made are between:

01/05/2013

and

01/05/2017

(3)  If a new factory is acquired for £200,000, the amount of the gain which can be rolled-over is:

£ | 55,760

| Gain immediately chargeable £(230,000 – 200,000) | 30,000 |
|---|---|
| Gain which can be rolled-over £(85,760 – 30,000) | 55,760 |

(b)

|  | ✓ |
|---|---|
| Troy will acquire the shop at a cost of £120,000. | ✓ |
| Sami will have no chargeable gain on the gift. | ✓ |
| The annual exempt amount is deducted before gift relief. |  |
| Troy will acquire the shop at a cost of £150,000. |  |

Troy will acquire the shop at MV less gift relief £(150,000 – 30,000), gift relief of £30,000 leaves Sami with no gain.

Gift relief cannot be restricted to allow Sami to use his annual exempt amount.

# BPP PRACTICE ASSESSMENT 4
# BUSINESS TAX

Time allowed: 2 hours

# Taxation Data

Taxation tables for Business Tax – 2014/15

Note that 'TAXATION DATA 1' and 'TAXATION DATA 2' shown below will be available as pop up windows throughout your live assessment.

## TAXATION DATA 1

*Capital allowances*
Annual investment allowance
| | |
|---|---|
| From 1 January 2013 | £250,000 |
| From 1/6 April 2014 | £500,000 |
| Plant and machinery writing down allowance | 18% |
| Motor cars | |
| $CO_2$ emissions up to 95g/km | 100% |
| $CO_2$ emissions between 96g/km and 130g/km | 18% |
| $CO_2$ emissions over 130g/km | 8% |
| Energy efficient and water saving plant | |
| First year allowance | 100% |

*Capital gains*
| | |
|---|---|
| Annual exempt amount | £11,000 |
| Standard rate | 18% |
| Higher rate (applicable over £31,865) | 28% |
| Entrepreneurs' relief rate | 10% |
| Entrepreneurs' relief limit | £10,000,000 |

*National insurance rates*
| | |
|---|---|
| Class 2 contributions: | £2.75 per week |
| Small earnings exception | £5,885 p.a. |
| Class 4 contributions: | |
| Main rate | 9% |
| Additional rate | 2% |
| Lower profits limit | £7,956 |
| Upper profits limit | £41,865 |

## TAXATION DATA 2

*Corporation tax*

| Financial year | 2014 | 2013 |
|---|---|---|
| Small profits rate | 20% | 20% |
| Marginal relief: | | |
| Lower limit | £300,000 | £300,000 |
| Upper limit | £1,500,000 | £1,500,000 |
| Standard fraction | 1/400 | 3/400 |
| Main rate | 21% | 23% |

Marginal relief formula: Fraction × (U–A) × N/A

# Business Tax BPP practice assessment 4

## Task 1

The statement of profit or loss Jeremy Ltd for the year to 31 March 2015 shows the following information:

|  | £ | £ |
| --- | --- | --- |
| Gross profit |  | 512,500 |
| Profit on sale of shares |  | 13,550 |
| Dividends received |  | 6,300 |
| Interest income |  | 4,500 |
|  |  | 536,850 |
| General expenses (Note 1) | 210,780 |  |
| Motor expenses (Note 2) | 40,500 |  |
| Wages and salaries | 110,350 |  |
| Administrative expenses | 77,230 |  |
| Depreciation charge | 15,700 |  |
|  |  | (454,560) |
| Profit for the year |  | 82,290 |

## Notes

(1) **General expenses**

These include:

|  | £ |
| --- | --- |
| Qualifying charitable donation (paid August 2014) | 500 |
| Entertaining customers | 9,550 |
| Entertaining staff | 8,650 |

(2) **Motor expenses**

These include:

|  | £ |
| --- | --- |
| Parking fines incurred by director | 610 |
| Petrol used by director for private use | 6,300 |
| Leasing costs of car for director ($CO_2$ emissions 180 g/km) | 9,300 |

(3) **Capital allowances**

The capital allowances for the year ended 31 March 2014 are £8,750.

**Using the proforma layout provided, compute the adjusted trading profit for Jeremy Ltd for the year to 31 March 2015. Fill in all unshaded boxes. Add a 0 (zero) if necessary.**

|  | £ | £ |
|---|---|---|
| Profit for the year per accounts |  | 82,290 |
|  | Add | Deduct |
| Profit on sale of shares |  |  |
| Dividends received |  |  |
| Interest income |  |  |
| Qualifying charitable donation |  |  |
| Entertaining customers |  |  |
| Entertaining staff |  |  |
| Parking fines incurred by director |  |  |
| Petrol used by director for private use |  |  |
| Leasing costs of car for director |  |  |
| Wages and salaries |  |  |
| Administrative expenses |  |  |
| Depreciation charge |  |  |
| Capital allowances |  |  |
| Total to add/deduct |  |  |
| Taxable trading profit |  |  |

## Task 2

Codie is in business as a sole trader making up accounts to 31 December each year. You have been asked to complete her capital allowances computation for the year to 31 December 2014. The following information is relevant:

(1) The capital allowance computation showed the following written-down value at 1 January 2014:

|  | £ |
|---|---|
| Main pool | 58,060 |

(2) During the period 1 January to 31 December 2014, Codie had the following capital transactions:

| Purchases | | £ |
|---|---|---|
| January 2014 | Plant and machinery | 5,030 |
| May 2014 | Plant and machinery | 441,750 |
| July 2014 | Car ($CO_2$ emissions 110g/km) | 19,320 (80% private use) |
| Disposals | | |
| January 2014 | Plant and machinery | 23,900 |

**Compute Codie's capital allowances computation for the year to 31 December 2014.**

| | | | | |
|---|---|---|---|---|
| | | | | |
| | | | | |
| | | | | |
| | | | | |
| | | | | |
| | | | | |
| | | | | |
| | | | | |
| | | | | |
| | | | | |
| | | | | |
| | | | | |
| | | | | |
| | | | | |
| | | | | |
| | | | | |
| | | | | |
| | | | | |

## Task 3

Xavier, Yvonne and Zebedee have been in partnership for many years making up accounts to 30 September each year. Under the partnership agreement, Xavier is entitled to a salary of £9,000 a year and the profits are then divided 2:2:1 between the partners respectively.

Xavier retired from the partnership on 31 December 2014. Yvonne and Zebedee carried on the partnership and the partnership agreement was altered so that the profits were then divided 2:1 between Yvonne and Zebedee respectively.

The partnership profits for the year to 30 September 2015 were £209,000.

(1) **Using the proforma layout provided, show the division of the partnership profit for the year to 30 September 2015. Fill in all unshaded boxes and add a 0 (zero) if necessary.**

| | Total £ | Xavier £ | Yvonne £ | Zebedee £ |
|---|---|---|---|---|
| **Period to 31/12/2014** | | | | |
| Salary | | | | |
| Share of profits | | | | |
| **Period to 30/09/2015** | | | | |
| Share of profits | | | | |
| Total profit for y/e 30/09/2015 | | | | |

You see from your files that Xavier's share of the partnership profit for the year to 30 September 2014 was £21,000 and that he had overlap profits of £4,500 on commencement.

(2) **Xavier's taxable partnership profits for the tax year of cessation are:**

£ [ ]

## Task 4

K Ltd decides to make up accounts for a 15 month period of account to 30 November 2014. Trading profits were £10,000 per month for the first 10 months and £12,000 per month thereafter. It made a capital gain of £10,000 in January 2014 and a capital gain of £20,000 in October 2014.

(a) **Identify whether the following statements are True or False.**

|  | True ✓ | False ✓ |
|---|---|---|
| The gain of £10,000 will be dealt with in the accounting period to 31 August 2014 and the gain of £20,000 will be dealt with in the accounting period to 30 November 2014. |  |  |
| Trading profits will be £124,000 in the accounting period to 31 August 2014 and £36,000 in the accounting period to 30 November 2014. |  |  |

A company has the following information for the year ended 31 March 2015:

* Taxable total profits are £250,000.
* Dividends received (net) are £13,500.
* The company has three associated companies.

(b) **Calculate the marginal relief that would apply.**

| Marginal relief for Finance Year 2014 | £ |
|---|---|
| 1/400 × [＿＿＿＿] − [＿＿＿＿] × [＿＿＿＿ / ＿＿＿＿] | [＿＿＿＿] |

---

## Task 5

Abdul is in business as a sole trader. His taxable trading profits for 2014/15 are £56,000, and he receives dividends of £9,000 in July 2014.

**The Class 2 NIC liability for 2014/15 is:**

£ [＿＿＿＿ . ＿＿]

**The Class 4 NIC liability for 2014/15 is:**

£ [＿＿＿＿ . ＿＿]

**The total NIC liability for 2014/15 is:**

| £ | | . | |
|---|---|---|---|

## Task 6

Osian makes a trading loss of £5,000 in 2014/15. He has property income of £6,300 in 2014/15. Osian had taxable trading income of £10,000 in 2013/14 and property income of £2,000.

(a) **Identify whether the following statements are True or False.**

| | True ✓ | False ✓ |
|---|---|---|
| Osian can claim to use his loss of 2014/15 against his general income in 2013/14 only, in order to preserve his personal allowance in 2014/15. | | |
| Osian can claim to use his loss of 2014/15 against his trading income in 2013/14 only, in order to preserve his personal allowance in 2014/15. | | |
| Osian must claim to use his loss of 2014/15 against his general income in 2014/15, before being able to carry it back. | | |

(b) **Identify whether the following statements are True or False for a company.**

| | True ✓ | False ✓ |
|---|---|---|
| When a trading loss is carried back by a company, it is set-off after deducting qualifying charitable donations. | | |
| A company can carry a trade loss back 12 months against total profits and forward 36 months against profits of the same trade. | | |
| A company must set-off trading losses in the current period before carrying back to the previous period. | | |

## Task 7

SR plc makes up accounts to 31 October each year. It pays tax at the small profits rate.

The corporation tax liability of SR plc for the year to 31 October 2014 was £24,000 and for the year to 31 October 2015 was £36,000.

(a) **How will SR plc pay the corporation tax liability for the year to 31 October 2015?**

|  | ✓ |
|---|---|
| 4 instalments of £6,000 each due on 14 May 2015, 14 August 2015, 14 November 2015 and 14 February 2016 with a balancing payment of £12,000 due on 14 April 2016 |  |
| One payment due on 31 January 2017 |  |
| 4 instalments of £9,000 each due on 14 May 2015, 14 August 2015, 14 November 2015 and 14 February 2016 |  |
| One payment due on 1 August 2016 |  |

(b) **Tick the appropriate box for each of the following statements.**

|  | True | False |
|---|---|---|
| The maximum penalty for an error in a tax return which is deliberate but not concealed is 75%. | ☐ | ☐ |
| If an individual submits his 2014/15 tax return online on 13 January 2016, HMRC can start an enquiry before 31 January 2017. | ☐ | ☐ |
| If a company submits its tax return two months late, the penalty is £100. | ☐ | ☐ |

## Task 8

**Complete the following extract from the tax return for Byatt Ltd for the year ended 31 March 2015, using the following information:**

|  | £ |
|---|---|
| Revenue | 320,000 |
| Trade profits | 215,000 |
| Chargeable gain | 18,000 |
| Qualifying charitable donation paid | 3,000 |
| Trading loss brought forward | (15,000) |
| Capital loss brought forward | (2,000) |

Page 2

# Company tax calculation

## Turnover

| | |
|---|---|
| 1 Total turnover from trade or profession | **1** £ |

## Income

| | |
|---|---|
| 3 Trading and professional profits | **3** £ |
| 4 Trading losses brought forward claimed against profits | **4** £ |
| 5 Net trading and professional profits | *box 3 minus box 4* **5** £ |
| 6 Bank, building society or other interest, and profits and gains from non-trading loan relationships | **6** £ |
| 11 Income from UK land and buildings | **11** £ |
| 14 Annual profits and gains not falling under any other heading | **14** £ |

## Chargeable gains

| | |
|---|---|
| 16 Gross chargeable gains | **16** £ |
| 17 Allowable losses including losses brought forward | **17** £ |
| 18 Net chargeable gains | *box 16 minus box 17* **18** £ |
| **21 Profits before other deductions and reliefs** | *sum of boxes 5, 6, 11, 14 & 18* **21** £ |

## Deductions and Reliefs

| | |
|---|---|
| 24 Management expenses under S75 ICTA 1988 | **24** £ |
| 30 Trading losses of this or a later accounting period under S393A ICTA 1988 | **30** £ |
| 31 Put an 'X' in box 31 if amounts carried back from later accounting periods are included in box 30 | **31** |
| 32 Non-trade capital allowances | **32** £ |
| 35 Charges paid | **35** £ |
| **37 Taxable total profits** | *box 21 minus boxes 24, 30, 32 and 35* **37** £ |

## Tax calculation

| | |
|---|---|
| 38 Franked investment income | **38** £ |
| 39 Number of associated companies in this period or | **39** |
| 40 Associated companies in the first financial year | **40** |
| 41 Associated companies in the second financial year | **41** |
| 42 Put an 'X' in box 42 if the company claims to be charged at the starting rate or the small companies' rate on any part of its profits, or is claiming marginal rate relief | **42** |

Enter how much profit has to be charged and at what rate of tax

| Financial year *(yyyy)* | Amount of profit | Rate of tax | Tax | |
|---|---|---|---|---|
| **43** | **44** £ | **45** | **46** £ | p |
| **53** | **54** £ | **55** | **56** £ | p |

| | |
|---|---|
| 63 Corporation tax | *total of boxes 46 and 56* **63** £ p |
| 64 Marginal rate relief | **64** £ p |
| 65 Corporation tax net of marginal rate relief | **65** £ p |
| 66 Underlying rate of corporation tax | **66** • % |
| 67 Profits matched with non-corporate distributions | **67** |
| 68 Tax at non-corporate distributions rate | **68** £ p |
| 69 Tax at underlying rate on remaining profits | **69** £ p |
| **70 Corporation tax chargeable** | *See note for box 70 in CT600 Guide* **70** £ p |

CT600 (Short) (2008) Version 2

## Task 9

FGH plc bought a painting in October 2008 for £3,600. FGH plc sold the painting at auction in September 2014 and received £7,200 after deducting the auctioneers' commission of £800. The indexation factor between October 2008 and September 2014 is 0.188.

(a) **Calculate the chargeable gain on the disposal of this asset.**                                        £

Proceeds

Disposal costs

Cost of acquisition

Indexation allowance

Gain

Gain using chattel marginal relief

Actual gain chargeable

(b) **For the following items of expenditure, tick if they are allowable when computing a capital gain:**

|  | Allowable | Not allowable |
| --- | --- | --- |
| Advertising for buyers | ☐ | ☐ |
| Repainting window frames | ☐ | ☐ |
| Stamp duty payable on acquisition | ☐ | ☐ |

## Task 10

Ros bought 2,000 shares in Blueberry Ltd for £10,000 in November 2006.

In March 2008, she received 400 shares in a bonus issue. In May 2010 the company offered a rights issue at 1 share for every 6 held. She accepted this rights issue at £3 per share. She sold 1,800 shares in Blueberry Ltd in July 2014 for £13,500.

**Using the proforma layouts provided, show the chargeable gain on sale.**

*Share pool*

|  | No of shares | Cost £ |
|---|---|---|
|  |  |  |
|  |  |  |
|  |  |  |
|  |  |  |
|  |  |  |
|  |  |  |
|  |  |  |

*Gain*

|  | £ |
|---|---|
| Proceeds of sale |  |
| Less allowable cost |  |
| Chargeable gain |  |

## Task 11

Three taxpayers sold similar assets during 2014/15 and each made a capital gain, after deducting their annual exemption (annual exempt amount), of £21,000. In the table below, the total of their other taxable income is shown.

**Show the amount of capital gain that would be chargeable under each of the two rates capital gains tax (CGT). You must enter 0 if your answer is zero.**

| Taxpayer | Other income (£) | Chargeable capital gain (£) | |
| --- | --- | --- | --- |
| | | 18% CGT rate | 28% CGT rate |
| Peter | 11,300 | | |
| Richard | 26,100 | | |
| Gemma | 66,800 | | |

# BPP PRACTICE ASSESSMENT 4
# BUSINESS TAX


# ANSWERS

# Business Tax BPP practice assessment 4

## Task 1

Jeremy Ltd adjusted trading profit for the year ending 31 March 2015.

|  | £ | £ |
| --- | --- | --- |
| Profit for the year per accounts |  | 82,290 |
|  | Add | Deduct |
| Profit on sale of shares | 0 | 13,550 |
| Dividends received | 0 | 6,300 |
| Interest income | 0 | 4,500 |
| Qualifying charitable donation | 500 | 0 |
| Entertaining customers | 9,550 | 0 |
| Entertaining staff | 0 | 0 |
| Parking fines incurred by director | 610 | 0 |
| Petrol used by director for private use | 0 | 0 |
| Leasing costs of car for director (£9,300 × 15%) | 1,395 | 0 |
| Wages and salaries | 0 | 0 |
| Administrative expenses | 0 | 0 |
| Depreciation charge | 15,700 | 0 |
| Capital allowances | 0 | 8,750 |
| Total to add/deduct | 27,755 | 33,100 |
| Taxable trading profit |  | 76,945 |

## Task 2

*Year ended 31 December 2014*

|  | AIA | Main pool | Car (20% business) | Allowances |
|---|---|---|---|---|
|  | £ | £ | £ | £ |
| B/f |  | 58,060 |  |  |
| *AIA additions* |  |  |  |  |
| January 2014 | 5,030 |  |  |  |
| May 2014 | 441,750 |  |  |  |
|  | 446,780 |  |  |  |
| Max AIA (w) | (437,500) |  |  | 437,500 |
| Transfer to main pool |  | 9,280 |  |  |
| Disposals |  | (23,900) |  |  |
| *Non-AIA addition* |  |  |  |  |
| Car |  |  | 19,320 |  |
|  |  | 43,440 |  |  |
| WDA @ 18% |  | (7,819) |  | 7,819 |
| WDA @ 18% |  |  | (3,478) × 20% | 696 |
|  |  | 35,621 | 15,842 | 446,015 |

(W) Maximum AIA

(£250,000 × 3/12 = £62,500) **plus** (£500,000 × 9/12 = £375,000) = £437,500

# Task 3

|  | Total £ | Xavier £ | Yvonne £ | Zebedee £ |
|---|---|---|---|---|
| **Period to 31/12/2014** |  |  |  |  |
| Salary (× 3/12) | 2,250 | 2,250 | 0 | 0 |
| Share of profits (2:2:1) | 50,000 | 20,000 | 20,000 | 10,000 |
| **Period to 30/09/2015** |  |  |  |  |
| Share of profits (2:1) | 156,750 | 0 | 104,500 | 52,250 |
| Total profit for y/e 30/09/2015 | 209,000 | 22,250 | 124,500 | 62,250 |

(2)  Xavier's taxable partnership profits for the tax year of cessation are:

| £ | 38,750 |
|---|---|

| 2014/15 | £ |
|---|---|
| Profit for y/e 30 September 2014 | 21,000 |
| Profit for p/e 31 December 2014 | 22,250 |
| Less overlap profit | (4,500) |
| Taxable profit for 2014/15 | 38,750 |

......................................................................................................

# Task 4

(a)  Identify whether the following statements are True or False.

|  | True ✓ | False ✓ |
|---|---|---|
| The gain of £10,000 will be dealt with in the accounting period to 31 August 2014 and the gain of £20,000 will be dealt with in the accounting period to 30 November 2014. | ✓ |  |
| Trading profits will be £124,000 in the accounting period to 31 August 2014 and £36,000 in the accounting period to 30 November 2014. |  | ✓ |

Trading profits will be £128,000 in the accounting period to 31 August 2014 and £32,000 in the accounting period to 30 November 2014, as they are time apportioned evenly.

(b)  Calculate the marginal relief that would apply.

| Marginal relief for Finance Year 2014 | | | | £ |
|---|---|---|---|---|
| 1/400 × | 375,000 | − 265,000 × | $\dfrac{250,000}{265,000}$ | 259 |

## Task 5

The Class 2 NIC liability for 2014/15 is:

| £ | 143 | • | 00 |
|---|---|---|---|

(£2.75 × 52)

The Class 4 NIC liability for 2014/15 is:

| £ | 3,334 | • | 52 |
|---|---|---|---|

£(41,865 − 7,956) × 9% + £(56,000 − 41,865) × 2%

The total NIC liability for 2014/15 is:

| £ | 3,477 | • | 52 |
|---|---|---|---|

## Task 6

(a)  Identify whether the following statements are True or False.

| | True ✓ | False ✓ |
|---|---|---|
| Osian can claim to use his loss of 2014/15 against his general income in 2013/14 only, in order to preserve his personal allowance in 2014/15. | ✓ | |
| Osian can claim to use his loss of 2014/15 against his trading income in 2013/14 only, in order to preserve his personal allowance in 2014/15. | | ✓ |
| Osian must claim to use his loss of 2014/15 against his general income in 2014/15, before being able to carry it back. | | ✓ |

(b) Identify whether the following statements are True or False for a company.

| | True ✓ | False ✓ |
|---|---|---|
| When a trading loss is carried back by a company, it is set-off after deducting qualifying charitable donations. | | ✓ |
| A company can carry a trading loss back 12 months against total profits and forward 36 months against profits of the same trade. | | ✓ |
| A company must set-off trading losses in the current period before carrying back to the previous period. | ✓ | |

When a trading loss is carried back by a company, it is set-off before deducting qualifying charitable donations.

When trade losses are carried forward there is no restriction, they are carried forward indefinitely.

......................................................................................

## Task 7

(a) How will SR plc pay the corporation tax liability for the year to 31 October 2015?

| | ✓ |
|---|---|
| 4 instalments of £6,000 each due on 14 May 2015, 14 August 2015, 14 November 2015 and 14 February 2016 with a balancing payment of £12,000 due on 14 April 2016 | |
| One payment due on 31 January 2017 | |
| 4 instalments of £9,000 each due on 14 May 2015, 14 August 2015, 14 November 2015 and 14 February 2016 | |
| One payment due on 1 August 2016 | ✓ |

(b) Tick the appropriate box for each of the following statements.

| | True | False |
|---|---|---|
| The maximum penalty for an error in a tax return which is deliberate but not concealed is 75%. | | ✓ (70%) |
| If an individual submits his 2014/15 tax return online on 13 January 2016, HMRC can start an enquiry before 31 January 2017. | | ✓ (return submitted by due date: 1 year from actual filing date) |
| If a company submits its tax return two months late, the penalty is £100. | ✓ | |

......................................................................................

# Task 8

|  | |
|------|------|
| Box 1 | £320000 |
| Box 3 | £215000 |
| Box 4 | £15000 |
| Box 5 | £200000 |
| Box 16 | £18000 |
| Box 17 | £2000 |
| Box 18 | £16000 |
| Box 21 | £216000 |
| Box 35 | £3000 |
| Box 37 | £213000 |
| Box 42 | X |
| Box 43 | 2014 |
| Box 44 | £213000 |
| Box 45 | 20% |
| Box 46 | £42600.00 |
| Box 63 | £42600.00 |
| Box 70 | £42600.00 |

........................................................................................

# Task 9

(a) Calculate the chargeable gain on the disposal of this asset.

|  | £ |
|------|------|
| Proceeds | 8,000 |
| Disposal costs | (800) |
| Cost of acquisition | (3,600) |
| Indexation allowance 0.188 × £3,600 | (677) |
| Gain | 2,923 |
| Gain using chattel marginal relief £(8,000 − 6,000) × 5/3 | 3,333 |
| Actual gain chargeable | 2,923 |

(b) For the following items of expenditure, tick if they are allowable when computing a capital gain:

| | Allowable | Not allowable |
|---|---|---|
| Advertising for buyers | ✓ | |
| Repainting window frames | | ✓<br>(revenue expense) |
| Stamp duty payable on acquisition | ✓ | |

## Task 10

*Share pool*

| | No of shares | Cost |
|---|---|---|
| | | £ |
| November 2006 Acquisition | 2,000 | 10,000 |
| March 2008 Bonus | 400 | nil |
| | 2,400 | 10,000 |
| May 2010 Rights 1 for 6 @ £3 | 400 | 1,200 |
| | 2,800 | 11,200 |
| July 2014 Disposal | (1,800) | (7,200) |
| c/f | 1000 | 4,000 |

*Gain*

| | £ |
|---|---|
| Proceeds of sale | 13,500 |
| Less allowable cost | (7,200) |
| Chargeable gain | 6,300 |

## Task 11

Show the amount of capital gain that would be chargeable under each of the two rates capital gains tax (CGT). You must enter 0 if your answer is zero.

| Taxpayer | Other income (£) | Chargeable capital gain (£) | |
|---|---|---|---|
| | | 18% CGT rate | 28% CGT rate |
| Peter | 11,300 | 20,565 | 435 |
| Richard | 26,100 | 5,765 | 15,235 |
| Gemma | 66,800 | 0 | 21,000 |

# TAXATION DATA

**Taxation tables for Business Tax – 2014/15**

**Note that 'TAXATION DATA 1' and 'TAXATION DATA 2' shown below will be available as pop up windows throughout your live assessment.**

## TAXATION DATA 1

*Capital allowances*
Annual investment allowance
    From 1 January 2013         £250,000
    From 1/6 April 2014         £500,000
Plant and machinery writing down allowance     18%
Motor cars
    $CO_2$ emissions up to 95g/km     100%
    $CO_2$ emissions between 96g/km and 130g/km     18%
    $CO_2$ emissions over 130g/km     8%
Energy efficient and water saving plant
    First year allowance     100%
*Capital gains*
Annual exempt amount     £11,000
Standard rate     18%
Higher rate (applicable over £31,865)     28%
Entrepreneurs' relief rate     10%
Entrepreneurs' relief limit     £10,000,000
*National insurance rates*
Class 2 contributions:     £2.75 per week
    Small earnings exception     £5,885 p.a.
Class 4 contributions:
    Main rate     9%
    Additional rate     2%
    Lower profits limit     £7,956
    Upper profits limit     £41,865

## TAXATION DATA 2

*Corporation tax*

| | 2014 | 2013 |
|---|---|---|
| *Financial year* | | |
| Small profits rate | 20% | 20% |
| Marginal relief: | | |
|   Lower limit | £300,000 | £300,000 |
|   Upper limit | £1,500,000 | £1,500,000 |
| Standard fraction | 1/400 | 3/400 |
| Main rate | 21% | 23% |

Marginal relief formula: Fraction × (U–A) × N/A

**Notes**